What People are saying about Frankie's Kingdom

When Deon prayed, "Lord, give them an understanding of grace, at any cost, even if we must be rejected in the process", he had no idea how costly the answer to that prayer would be. Out of rejection from the kingdom of religion, God has been honing the message of His grace and His glorious kingdom in Deon and Susan. Now you have the privilege of participating in Deon's journey, discovering that a relationship with our Father is infinitely more personal and empowering when it is not encumbered by the damaging protocol of a religious system. In 2000 and 2001, Bev and I returned to South Africa for an 18 month period. Deon and I spent many hours in restaurants overlooking East London's beach-front discussing issues of grace, the new covenant, the kingdom of God and the application of these truths to life. In Frankie's Kingdom you will hear the passion of Deon's heart and join him in the journey of discovering your position and possessions as sons in the Father's kingdom.

John Sheasby, Liberated Living Ministries, Tulsa, Oklahoma, USA

Deon Stevens brings a clear perspective of our distinctiveness as dearly loved sons, set apart to live with an unfair advantage. Our princely identity reveals our royal standing, our indisputable authority, making the enemy's intimidation seem trivial. We share the very same miraculous glory that Jesus displayed on the Earth—our gloriousness defined in our heavenly Father's gloriousness.

Errol Petersen, Retired Pastor, Greenfields Christian Church

Burdened under the yoke of religion? This book will challenge you to get out of the rut of the religious paradigms we get into so easily. Deon Stevens challenges us to review what we believe and live a life of abundant flow in God's Grace. Some things will shock, some you will want to debate, but if read with an open heart and open mind, you like me, will be spurred onto loving Jesus and people more and allowing the Holy Spirit to live Christ's abundant life in and through you.

Brian Bennets, Pastor, Eastern Cape, South Africa

Frankie's Kingdom gives compelling evidence that we are actually like Jesus and dearly loved by Him. In understanding this, we come to a place of incredible liberty, victory and freedom. The degree that we dare to break free from the trap of religiosity will determine the degree to which we will find true acceptance and victory through Jesus Christ who is passionately in love with us. If read with an open mind, Frankie's Kingdom can bring new conviction, fresh purpose and extraordinary joy to your life.

Roy Stevens, Pastor, East London, South Africa

Frankie's Kingdom

Winning in Face of Uncertainty

Deon Stevens

Revised Edition

ISBN 978-0-620-39080-4

Revised Edition

Dedication

This book is dedicated to one of my true heroines. She was dealt a double whammy, neither of which were of her own making.

It was September 2006. Our family had gathered from the four corners of the Globe at my sister's beach house on the Wild Coast of South Africa, to celebrate our daughter, Jacqui's marriage to Al. They were down from Dubai. Andy and Michele had flown in from New Zealand. Michael, Carmen Dylan and Tyla were down from Kimberley and Susan and I, from Cape Town. It's not every day that our scattered family gets together. What a joy! A rare treasure!

We were privileged to share the occasion with our extended family— thirty-two of us in all. Such a blessing!

The subtropical Wild Coast sunshine, the pristine beach and lagoon, the shared affection of a loving family—we could not have wished for a more idyllic moment in paradise.

The warm family gathering ended with goodbyes, hugs and kisses. But did it really have to end this way?

"Emma has Leukaemia!" Our blissful holiday suddenly shocked into reality—what a blow! This can't be happening to our little darling. How dare such a dreaded diagnosis choose our precious seven-year-old niece? The upbeat atmosphere turned to gloom. We needed answers, we needed comfort—but who to turn to? At times like this, we don't know the answers, but there is one who does—He's our heavenly Father!

This was by no means the first setback in this sweet kid's life. She was born deaf, and with the help of the world's best parents and Cochlea Implants, she had valiantly turned her disability into a triumph. Now leukaemia—as if deafness wasn't enough for this little mite to cope with. What could be more challenging than deafness? How about staying alive! Why do bad things happen to good people?

During Emma's Chemotherapy, she overheard the specialist telling her Mom that she can expect Emma to have the worst kind of nightmares while under anaesthesia for a lumber punch. But when Emma woke, she told her Mom that she had not had nightmares, but a very lovely dream. She dreamt about people dressed in white. Her Mom left it at that but couldn't help wondering what the dream was all about, so she asked Emma. Emma told the most amazing story!

"A white staircase went all the way to the sky. At the top was a big chair full of jewels. Angels dressed in white were coming down the stairs with flowers and presents for me, one carried a silver crown with feathers on a cushion. They massaged my legs and gave me fruit juice to drink."

Isn't our God really cool? Emma's dream touched our hearts with a fresh reminder of God's loving grace. Just a brief glimpse into the spiritual realm, and we discover a love so much greater than we could ever imagine.

While this book is by no means a child's story, the simplicity of God's love can be understood by anyone of any age.

Emma, our little sweetheart, what an inspiration you are!

Enjoying a moment with our precious Emma

Acknowledgements

I am always amazed at how God seems to guide me to the right material and people, once I take the plunge to begin writing a book.

On a visit to Peter and Sandy Meyer in Freemantle, Australia, I began reading a book I found on Sandy's coffee table. She told me that I had better read fast—I could not take it home to South Africa—it belonged to someone else. As I read it, I realised that it was no accident. The book explained the difficult concepts I was grappling with. I simply had to have a copy of my own.

The next morning, we set out for the Koorong bookshop in central Perth. We drove part of the way, took a ferry and a few busses. What a great bookstore, but what a let-down to discover that the book was not in stock. Disappointed, we turned to leave, and to our surprise, literally bumped into Sandy's friend, the owner of the original copy. Sandy explained my predicament. Her immediate response was, "Please let Deon keep my copy."

Sandy's friend, who also lived in Freemantle, would probably only visit the store a couple of times a year. I have only been there once and will probably never get back to it. If the timing of either of our visits to the store were only a few seconds out, we would not have bumped into each other. As always, God's timing is immaculate. The chance of us meeting at such a remote spot was probably a gazillion to one. Doubtless, the meeting had been divinely ordained.

The book? Steve McVey's 'Grace Land'. The sheer impossibility of "doing what Christ would do" in all circumstances is easily solved when we give up trying to be like Jesus and simply allow the indwelling Christ to effortlessly live His life through our lives. No effort is required as we relax and watch Him at work through our actions—our behaviour becomes Christ-like without trying.

The right people would cross my path at exactly the right time, helping me to understand difficult concepts as and when they arose.

While doing my research for this book, there was another concept that I was struggling with. I asked the Lord to clarify this point. A few days later I walked into a bookstore, wondering which book would hold the answer. There were thousands of titles. I had no idea where to begin? I randomly pulled a book from one of the many shelves, aimlessly flipped it open to page 126, and steering me in the face was the precise answer to my question. The author was not known to me. This could only have been God's guidance. In my own wisdom, I would never have given this author so much as a second glance.

Again, overwhelmed with gratitude, I knew I was on track! Nothing could be sweeter than being led by the Holy Spirit. Everything seemed to slot in perfectly on time with faultless precision. What a delight to see His stamp of approval on the project?

When I told the bookstore manager of my good fortune, his answer to me was, "And they say there is no God?" What an awesome God we serve!

The book? 'Is God to blame?' Gregory Boyd's book provided more conformation—I knew with absolute certainty that I was heading in the right direction. Much of what God directed me to write about is seldom, if ever taught. What are the chances of stumbling upon such a remote subject by chance?

Of course, it is easy to say that the Bible is the final authority, but how could I be sure that my understanding of these Biblical concepts was correct? Gregory's in-depth understanding of the scriptures reassured me that my view was not at all offbeat. The concept that I was wrestling with was the significance of the fruit of the tree of the knowledge of good and evil in the Garden of Eden. The book also helped me to gain a clearer picture of God's will—how it is allowed or disallowed by mere mortals. Then there are the questions, "Is God to blame for the bad things that come our way? Does He cause bad things to happen to us for our ultimate good, or should we be placing the blame elsewhere?"

Does this information really have any bearing on day-to-day living? You bet it does! We need to know the authority God has vested in us— what rights He has given us and what role we play in establishing His Kingdom on earth. Without this information, we may be needlessly putting up with Satan's harassments. Our arch enemy is out to get us, and he is merciless! If we are not entirely convinced of our authority over him, he will use our ignorance to disrupt God's glorious plan for our lives. Unless we are convinced that we can dominate and disrupt Satan's agenda, he will dominate and disrupt our agenda. That being the case, what authority do we actually have over him? If we are to believe that he only has as much leeway as we allow, then how should we curtail his wicked agenda to kill, steal and destroy?

There is no way around it—the moment we become children of God, the war begins. Too many Christians have opted not to join the fray, oblivious to the fact that warfare is not optional, we are in a war whether we like it or not! What is optional though, is whether we allow Satan to walk all over us—he is out to dictate unhappiness and to destroy peace. Many are comfortable with passivity; not comprehending the coastal cost! Believe me, they will be required to pay for it! The question arises: How much are we prepared to lose before taking action? For as long as we allow him to get away with killing, stealing and destroying, our treasured peace and contentment will remain at stake. Although we are at war, we do not fight with anything more than words declared in faith. Declarations enforce the indisputable victory that Jesus accomplished for us on the cross.

Ask Christians how they are, and you are likely to get the reply, "Well, under the circumstances, not too bad." So many believers live under their circumstances, not knowing the power and authority they possess to live above them. To them high victory is a wonderful concept taught on Sundays, but sadly, never actually experienced Monday through Saturday.

Andre Rabe's insightful perceptions on sonship in his book Adventures in Christ, helped to clarify some of my views regarding our relationship with our Father.

Contents

Foreword

Rob Rufus, Pastor of City Church International Hong Kong.

I love reading whatever inspires hope and confidence. This powerful book has the flair of making you aware of how good God really is! You need never be bullied by lies again.

As I read through the pages I felt thoroughly equipped to condemn condemnation, to accuse accusation, to grab guilt by the throat, to get out of the boat and float, and to wear the Glory coat.

Perceiving one-self to be under condemnation from God, Satan or people usually results in self-condemnation. To the degree that you get rid of self-condemnation—to that degree the Glory of God manifests in your life. Much self-condemnation equals very little Glory Presence, little self-condemnation equals some Glory Presence, no self-condemnation equals the Full Glory Presence! God's abundant blessing is in His Glory.

Deon Stevens has seen this and has understood the crippling effects that condemnation has had on the Church. For centuries condemnation has spread itself over God's people like a damp sack, suffocating hope. Deon has diagnosed the problem accurately and with heavenly insights is trumpeting the call to freedom and confidence before God through Grace alone.

I believe that Deon is a strategic champion of a Glorious Grace revolution taking place throughout the earth. This is not a book of empty froth, bubbles and shadows, but has the substance of rich unveiled truth, unfolding in a supernatural sequence of liberating revelation that will set your heart racing with joy and inspire a fresh love for Jesus. All things are possible to a people set free from uncertainty, confusion and condemnation.

Thank you so much Deon for your courage and compassion. I honor you and salute you in His abundant Grace.

Preface

I feel as though I have spent a lifetime in church. At times I wondered if I was there purely because I was trying to impress people, and at other times, to impress God. Neither of these motivations were in any way appropriate.

I was taught that I would be rewarded for my faithfulness, so I obediently put myself through the boredom of more meetings. It seemed to me that church people had less fun than non-churchgoers. My friends were out in the sunshine, surfing and skiing, enjoying God's creation, while I was dragging myself through the torture of yet another dreary sermon. I would secretly keep an eye on my watch, willing it on, drifting off, daydreaming, anything to pass the time—seeking a more pleasurable subject to muse upon while the preacher did his best to hold my attention.

We were regularly told that we had the joy of the Lord and so should let our faces know how happy we were. This seemed like a farce to me. Surely, if we were truly happy, there would be no need to convince our faces.

We were told that, unless we shaped up, our Christianity was in question. It seemed to me that staying saved had something to do with our performance. I couldn't help thinking that church was missing the point. It felt as though the life of a Christian was about endless striving for holiness without the faintest hope of actually achieving it. The only achievement was the feeling of failure and guilt for repeatedly disappointing God.

I witnessed to people to keep my conscience happy, but secretly hoped that they would not find out where I went to church. I didn't want them to discover the emptiness of Christian striving.

The church regularly blamed the disappointments of life on the sovereignty of God. "God knows best," they would say. It appeared to me that there wasn't much point to prayer if God could sovereignly decide otherwise. I was told that God had His favourites—obviously I was not one of them.

Holiness had something to do with no dancing, no movies, no drinking, no smoking, no long hair—all-in-all no fun! For women, no make-up, no slacks, no short hair—buns were in fashion—ugliness was the order of the day, in fact, ugly seemed to equal holiness.

We could never get too familiar with one another. We addressed each other by surnames prefaced with "brother" or "sister". It always had to be Brother Smith and Sister Jones; it couldn't be Joe and Sally. Congregants were never too familiar with our Minister—always officially referring to him as "Pastor". All these titles served only to keep us at arm's length from each other—friendships consigned to shallowness.

Tithing was done to keep us from being cursed. All-in-all we paid a lot of money just to have someone beat us up with more guilt Sunday after Sunday. I cannot kid you, Hymns were a drag and sermons a yawn!

Jesus was kind, but God the Father was severe, stern and harsh, and the Holy Ghost was easily offended. Being a Christian was like walking on eggshells—being carefree was unacceptable. There was more emphasis on the fear of God than on a relationship with Him. Joy was a subject often spoken about, but not something anybody seemed to experience.

Then one day, too my surprise, God changed. No longer was He strict and unapproachable! Suddenly, He was gentle. He no longer had any favourites. He allowed us the freedom to exercise our will. He didn't keep a record of our wrongdoings. We could fellowship with Him without making any promises to change. We could approach Him boldly in our time of need. He had delegated power and authority to us. We were loved! Don't tell me that God cannot change—but of course He hadn't changed at all—it was I who had changed. What made the difference? In a word, "GRACE!"

Now that my concept of God had changed, I began to confront the religious fetters that had held me bound hand and foot for so long. The more I examined the shackles of religion, the more certain I became that religion achieves the exact opposite of what it sets out to achieve. The more religion, the less intimacy with our heavenly Father. Religion only serves to keep God at arm's length—forever out of reach. The sheer pleasure of entering His presence boldly is just not possible when religion has reduced us to undoneness! No amount of religious gymnastics can make up for what we lack in intimacy with the King. But here is the good news: We don't have to qualify ourselves! That's all over and done with. Jesus did it for us!

Religion and intimacy with the Father simply don't mix. Some influential church dudes from the distant past, who failed to experience the overcoming life that Jesus had promised, made up a bunch of religious rules to compensate for their lack of the supernatural. If they could not have genuine intimacy with God, then at least they could practice a ritual that mimicked the real deal. As repugnant as this was to God, these rules have enslaved God's kids throughout the ages—subjecting the devout to meaningless formulas and empty religion. To this day, sincere believers are still caught up in this charade.

If we can't have the real deal, at least church attendance provides an opportunity to discharge our religious duty for the week—a conscience appeasement. Is God impressed? I think not! But nobody seems brave enough to admit it. Let's be honest, religion provides comfort, albeit false comfort!

If you are religious, you may find the rest of this book distasteful. What I have to say runs roughshod over the notion that we can earn favour from God through good works. Why would anybody want to put themselves through the grind, when they are already favoured and in supremely good standing with their heavenly Dad. His Son has left us an extravagant inheritance. No need to chase after it with religion's many formulas when we have been invited to take ownership of it with nothing more than faith.

Nobody seems to have an explanation as to how He could be delighted with kids as delinquent as His. It seems obvious to me that He delights in their delight of His love for them. How delightful for us to return love to Him, not because we must, but because we really want to. There could only be one reason for loving Him, and that is that we have discovered how deeply we are loved. Let's be honest, could legalistic rules and religious structures possibly add anything to a romance that is already perfect?

I have often asked myself why He gives me concepts to write about that challenge traditional thought. There are so many safe topics that don't offend religious minds. Why can't I write about them? Maybe it's because I am not afraid to test anything I am expected to believe.

Why this book? I desperately want others to discover His magnificent love for them. The sheer delight of an intimate loving relationship with the Father bears absolutely no resemblance to the tedious boredom of religion. Allow me to share the joy of God's love with you. It is contrary to all the religious mumbo jumbo that had held me captive for so many years. I have had about as much as I can stomach from the bondage of performance-based Christianity. In God's perfect plan, there is no place for religious antics. What business does churchified legalism have in a divine romance—what can it possibly add to something that is already perfect? Hierarchical religious structures and surreptitious clerical manipulations veiled in a Christianese language that has nothing in the world to do with Christianity, is regularly foisted upon the unsuspecting.

I have been there long enough to understand exactly what others are going through. I hate watching them blindly stumbling down the same slippery path to nothing but a devotion to empty religion and unfulfilled dreams.

In these pages, I trust that you will find that connecting with God is simple, without religious yokes, pious handcuffs or self-righteous-making leg shackles. Satan has surreptitiously slipped these bondages into religion to enslave God's precious children. Although intended to regulate behaviour, they succeed only to hinder our heavenly Papa from delighting in the fatherly privilege of being a Daddy to His beloved children.

As you rediscover the extent of His love for you, I trust that you will draw from it, and as you do, discover that you are empowered to achieve so much more. In discovering where God has drawn the line upon His sovereignty, you will discover new horizons to your personal sovereignty and dominion over life's many hurdles. My prayer for you is that you will discover that God is not to blame for the chaos in the world and in your life, and that this knowledge will reinforce your trust in Him. More than anything, I trust that you will grasp God's undying love for you in a way that you may not have known before!

DISCLAIMER: This book carries a strong warning. The information contained in it can only be accommodated in new wineskins. It is dangerous for old wineskins to be exposed to new wine. The fermentation process requires elasticity to accommodate the effervescent joy of God's new wine. Beware! Religious wineskins will burst—His love is ever expanding.

The author takes no responsibility for burst wineskins. It is strongly recommended that old wine skins read no further! However, if they dare, it is recommended that their skins first be softened and revitalised with the oil of the Holy Spirit.

When the author began to understand that God's undying relationship with His children is meant to be unfettered by religiousness, it challenged some of his cherished Christian non-negotiables, offending him almost to the point of bursting his wineskin. Though it seriously rocked his boat, he discovered new stability on the troubled waters of life in the truths he gained concerning God's grace. But before stability was reached, a process of reinvigoration of the oil of the Holy Spirit had to be applied, making it possible for him to safely accommodate the un-religiousness of God's new wine.

We are not to be broad-minded, accommodating the world's way of thinking, but be open-minded to the Holy Spirit's leading; even if it means discarding our holy cows. Major church denominations exist for the sole reason that they camped at the last move of God, thereby becoming enemies of God's next move. God progressively reveals Himself to His church in stages—we can choose to camp at our last revelation of Him or continue to move with His glorious cloud.

Imperfect Judgement

Frankie, the first frog, started his life in a muddy little pool. To a frog nothing could be finer. The puddle was all that Frankie knew. Nobody told him that the world was bigger than the puddle. There was an ample supply of insect delicacies and the water was great for splashing around. "Croak, croak!" Frankie was blissfully unaware of a life any better than his cherished puddle. Here Frankie was in charge. This was Frankie's kingdom—Frankie's Garden of Eden—sheer bliss!

Then one day Stevie, the snake, came by and convinced Frankie that he was deceived. There was more to the world than the puddle. In fact, there was a great big swamp out there with many more insects—much juicier ones! "When you get there, your mind will be enlightened, and you will know just how wrong you have been all these years." Stevie was very convincing. Before Frankie could blink, he had been talked into swapping the little puddle for the promise of a huge swamp.

As Frankie ventured out beyond the edge of the puddle; to His disappointment, he discovered the swamp to be fraught with danger. He had to compete with other creatures—dangerous creatures for a measly lunch of dead flies lying in the mud around the smelly swamp. That's when the cold reality of his deception sank in—life here was sheer hell! The peace he once knew had become no more than a distant memory. And to top it all, he was no longer in charge. He had entered someone else's kingdom.

No problem for Frankie, he could always return to the puddle and recapture his lost piece of paradise. Problem was, the puddle now belonged to someone else, and Frankie didn't have the strength to take Stevie on and survive the encounter. He needed help—someone who could overpower Stevie.

In the meantime, Frankie went on to have a family. Unfortunately, he passed on to his children the wrong thinking that had gotten him into trouble. Equipped with this deception, one of his sons unfairly judged and sentenced his brother to death. And so, Stevie's evil legacy was passed on from generation to generation in perpetuity.

Frankie's dilemma became the dilemma of all frog-kind. No frog was able to reverse their ancestor's blunder.

"And the LORD God planted all sorts of trees in the garden— beautiful trees that produced delicious fruit. In the centre of the garden were two trees: the tree of life and the tree of the knowledge of good and evil. …the LORD God gave him this warning: "You may freely eat any fruit in the garden except fruit from the tree of the knowledge of good and evil. If you eat of its fruit, you will surely die" (Gen 2:9, 16, 17).

Kenny Waters walked into court a convicted killer, having served almost 20 years of a life sentence. He walked out a free man.

Eighteen years earlier, Waters was found guilty of beating and stabbing to death Katharina Brow during a 1980 robbery. His defence crumbled when the jury chose to believe a former lover's testimony rather than his.

"I told them, 'I didn't kill nobody man! I don't know what you people are talking about' ".

His lawyer at the time argued that Waters had been in court on the morning in question. This should have been an iron-clad alibi. The trouble was that nobody in Massachusetts believed him. Well, practically nobody. His sister believed him. She was a high school drop-out, with two kids, no job and a crazy idea.

In Betty Ann Waters' own words, "I think I'm going to law school" and that exited Kenny. He just said "Yes!"

Ms Waters had a big plan, but also a lot of doubts about taking on such an enormous challenge, but Kenny's faith in his kid sister kept her on course.

"I knew how smart she was", Kenny Waters said.

It took Betty Ann Waters twelve long years to graduate from law school. She just doggedly persisted until eventually she succeeded.

Inside prison, Kenny's despair nearly led to his death as he attempted suicide—anything to end his frustration. Outside, his sister just kept digging. She had graduated from law school specifically to prove her brother's innocence and to obtain his freedom. Since graduating, she has had very little use for her legal qualification. Twelve long years of dogged devotion to studying was purely for Kenny's benefit.

The breakthrough came when she hounded a clerk at the courthouse and learned of a box of evidence with her brother's name on it in the basement. The box contained the blood-stained knife used in the slaying, and a few pieces of bloody cloth. She enlisted the help of the "Innocence Project", a group that helps inmates challenge past convictions with DNA evidence. The material was tested, and the district attorney's office announced that the DNA did not match her brother's. After 20 long years, her brother was set free.

"I'm just really happy my brother is sitting next to me right now. It's not real yet", she said.

In March 2001, Kenny Waters was the 85th prisoner in America to be released because of contradictory DNA evidence, but he didn't thank the judicial system, he didn't even thank science, he thanked his sister!

"Sisters are the best things in the world. Always take care of your sisters. They'll take care of you", he said.

There is a sad twist to this story. Six months after his release, he died in an accident. The best part of his life had been wasted in a lonely prison cell, all because of a faulty judgement. The judicial system had failed Kenny Waters. He was freed because of the critical clues hidden in his blood, and the persistence of someone who never stopped believing in him. Kenny lost his reputation and 20 long years of his life, all because of the faulty judgement of imperfect men.

One of the surprising revelations of recent times is the number of rape and murder convictions that have been overturned after DNA evidence proved the convicts to be innocent. The Innocence Project has overturned 197 cases to date. These innocent prisoners had spent an average of 12 years behind bars—fourteen of them had been sentenced to death.

Getting a judgement overturned is all well and good, but how does the poor unfortunate individual get his many lost years back? Half of Kenny's life was wasted in a lonely prison cell. With doubts of his innocence in the minds of his family and friends and all respect for him long gone, how could life ever be what it was meant to be? To compound matters, he was consigned to live out the rest of his days with psychological hang-ups—a mind damaged by years of prison abuse and torturous solitude. One wonders how many other innocent men and women will have to sit out unjust sentences all because no DNA evidence was left behind to prove their innocence.

Given this sad judicial record, you would probably feel very insecure if you were falsely accused. Imagine being charged with a murder you didn't commit. You couldn't be sure whether you would get an impartial or prejudiced judge and jury. Let's face it, all people are influenced in some way by the sum total of their life's experiences. Subconscious prejudices develop over time. And judges, being mere mortals, are not immune.

Like court judges, everybody makes judgements upon others in their everyday lives. I remember the times when I was wrongly accused by my father for my brother's misdemeanours, and other times when my brother was accused of mine. But was it ever God's intention for mankind to gain the ability to judge one another?

Among the magnificent trees in the Garden of Eden, two were given special mention—the tree of life and the tree of the knowledge of good and evil. God told Adam and Eve to eat the fruit from any tree except from the tree of the knowledge of good and evil. Why did God make an issue of its fruit? It was because He did not want the perfect relationship He enjoyed with Adam and his wife to be spoiled by a Godless judgement of right and wrong. He knew that such insight would invoke a sense of shame, capable of driving a wedge between God and man. Imperfect men are only capable of making imperfect judgements, skewed by prejudice. Offense taking and critical spirits would ruin perfectly good friendships.

For the first time ever, they would have reason to accuse and lay blame upon one another. Relationships were at risk of being damaged, at times, beyond repair. Most damaging of all would be the loss of a perfect relationship between Heavenly Father and His beloved toddlers. God refers to such separation as spiritual death.

Before eating the fruit of the knowledge of good and evil, Adam and Eve had absolutely no knowledge of, not even the slightest inkling that such a concept as good and evil even existed. To them everything just existed—they didn't perceive good or bad in anything. As God's children, they were blissfully unaware of anything that could possibly come between them and their Heavenly Father.

Neither Adam nor Eve ever once looked at each other in judgement. They had no measure, such as the law, by which to judge one another. Concepts of innocence and guilt, blame and forgiveness, were completely foreign to their understanding. Repentance was a concept beyond their comprehension—such a notion had never even occurred to them. They simply enjoyed sweet fellowship with one another and with their heavenly Father. They didn't know anything else—there was no shame to inhibit the sweet fellowship they enjoyed with each other and their heavenly Father. None of their actions were judged by Him. Their lack of this knowledge ensured that their perfect union could not be clouded by offence taking and imperfect judgements. Their relationships with one another, and with their heavenly Father was in no way impeded by a consciousness of shame.

Then one day this innocence was rudely interrupted. Satan put doubt in Eve's mind about the trustworthiness of God, enticing her to do the one and only forbidden thing—eat the fruit of the knowledge of good and evil. The moment she and Adam ate it, an enlightenment dawned upon them. Suddenly, what they had thought to be perfect, was not at all perfect. A new concept was born—the awfulness of judgementalism! In the process of seeing one another's faults, they would also discover their own faults. Guilt would cause them to experience something never before known to mankind—personal shame! This would make them feel unworthy of God's love—undeserving of an intimate relationship with their heavenly Father. For the first time, they experienced feelings of extreme unease and discomfort in His presence. This shame would be passed down from generation to generation. People would eventually feel so uneasy in God's presence that they would ask Moses to meet with God on their behalf—unwilling to face God in their disgrace. This shame avoiding tactic of hiding behind the clergy, in preference to a vital first-hand relationship with God, continues to be the preferred practice of many modern-day believers.

Why did God shield Adam from knowing the difference between good and evil? In God's perfect plan for mankind, judgement was entirely unnecessary. Besides, He could not trust imperfect beings to decide on the degree of another person's imperfection. God knew that fair judgement can only be exercised from a standpoint of personal perfection, such as His own. Judgement from a position of imperfection could only produce imperfect conclusions. No human would ever be able to handle this responsibility fairly.

It is no different in our day and age. No matter how pure our motives may be, we just don't have the capacity to handle a responsibility as crucial as judging others with any degree of fairness. God knew that the knowledge gained would manifest in flawed judgements, skewed by personal prejudice. We would see others through spectacles distorted by personal bias developed through countless wounds inflicted by life's many unfair twists and turns—layer upon layer of bigotry and prejudice would form social scars and calluses. These biases, hidden from us in the fathomless recesses of our subconscious minds, would manifest in the most appalling ways. With inherent blind spots, we deny, deny, deny! We are convinced that we are better than those we judge—we are right, and they are wrong, and that's all there is to it!

For some, the appearance of a person, their body piercings and tattoos, or lack thereof, or perhaps the colour of their skin, may influence opinions. For others, it may be the egotistical self-centred behaviour of a person that gives reason for despisement. We don't take the trouble to discern what led to such self-absorbedness. There may be underlying reasons for their attention seeking self-centeredness, but we are not about to give him or her a second chance. To us, such a person deserves nothing more than a cold shoulder. Their obnoxious attitude is sufficient reason to prejudice them. We feel that by ignoring them and their constant self-seeking demands for approval, we will be teaching them a lesson, so we give them the brush-off! Though we have the antidote to the poison that has distorted their thinking; we choose to snub them. In this way, our warped judgement continues to wound the wounded!

If we only considered for a moment, we would see that the wounds that cause this kind of behaviour are the very wounds that Jesus came to heal. It was the broken hearts, the bruised reeds that He promised not to break, and the smoking flax that He would not snuff out. He came to set captives free—His touch healed, and His words encouraged. The only ones for which Jesus had any strong words, were for self-righteous judgemental people—the religious mob—the Pharisees and their ilk. He had mercy and grace for everybody else!

Some of our partialities originate in cultural preferences. For others it could be a person's music preference, political affiliation or denomination that causes the scales to tip against them. In its most innocent form, we choose sport heroes based on how they fit in with our personal belief system.

Whether Christian or not, our choices are often slanted—unable to see eye to eye, at odds with one another—all for what? Prejudices so easily drive wedges between the best of friends. Personal political preferences are prime examples of bad judgement. With such divergent points of view, it doesn't take a rocket scientist to know that we can't all be right.

During my national service I was often the recipient of a thousand angry words from the NCOs on the parade ground for no other reason than that I was English-speaking in an Afrikaans-speaking world. I was addressed as "Engelsman", (Englishman—a derogatory word among Afrikaaners). A word that was spat out in disdain! Prejudice was commonplace in the army. The English-speakers had their own derogatory word for Afrikaners: "Dutchmen!" Each group had stereotyped the other, resulting in their judgements being horribly skewed by the assumption that if one person in the opposite group was intellectually challenged, then everybody in that group were imbeciles! Obviously, on the basis of such bias, neither group's judgements could be trusted.

By contrast, God's judgement can never be wrong—always fair! But for us, the knowledge of good and evil has a way of distorting our conclusions.

God knew, that given the ability to judge, even best friends would find reason never to speak to each other again. Fathers would disown their rebellious children. Offended brothers would avoid each other. Mothers would desert their families for convenient reasons. Pastors would be put on the street by the very people they committed their lives to serve. Judgement would justify divorce, abortion and betrayal. In its worst form, it would validate the genocide of six million Jews, the ethnic cleansing of a million Rwandans, and the mass murder of thousands of innocent hardworking moms and dads on 9/11.

We may not stoop to such depths of depravity, but we may carry offences and unforgiveness to our graves. By God's measure, these secret grudges are no less evil than the most gruesome acts of terrorism perpetrated on innocent women and children.

Our judgement will always be skewed, instigating secret grudge bearing, hidden anger and bitterness—all self-destructive emotions—more damaging to ourselves than to the people we begrudge. Bitterness towards others makes a meal of our peace—denying any possibility of happiness. Bitterness is poison, not to the offender, but to the offended. We drink it in the hope that the person we detest will die. But they live on happily, while we succumb to the noxious brew intended for them.

Precious families are torn apart, and good friendships destroyed. Damaged egos retaliate with even fiercer judgement than the judgement they receive. One person's revenge stoking the fires of another's revenge!

Nothing can wound more deeply than the searing judgement of a close friend. Rightly or wrongly, both parties get hurt—at times, relationships are irreparably trashed! We may not always express our judgement, but often undertones of wounded spirits betray seemingly innocent conversations—suppressed anger and revengeful thoughts lurk just below the surface.

And when things go wrong, God is often judged. From a position of imperfection, men and women are brazen enough to accuse a perfect God. When bad things happen to good people, blame is often laid at His door. They might not say it in so many words. It is usually cloaked in religious Christianese like: "God allowed this for a purpose"; "God is teaching you a lesson"; "God is trying your faith" or "God is punishing you because He loves you". With this approach, no matter how we couch our accusations, it is God we are accusing.

A drunken driver kills an innocent child riding her tricycle in the apparent safety of a sidewalk. They ask, "Why did God allow it? Why didn't He prevent it?" They believe this distortion and conclude that it is His doing—His fault! But surely it is obvious—He cannot be blamed for man's flawed decisions!

With legalism, holiness is defined by do's and don'ts. While visible behaviour is managed, wayward thinking remains unchallenged. Sadly, supposedly less heinous sins like offense taking and gossip go under the radar. Such sins are certainly not harmless. Disguised gracelessness is immensely destructive to relationships—dividing friendships, hurting the very ones who have thrived on our love and acceptance.

"Hypocrite! First get rid of the log from your own eye; then perhaps you will see well enough to deal with the speck in your friend's eye" (Mat 7:5). That was Jesus' caution to us. Jesus is not giving us permission to judge others once we have dealt with the log in our own eye. He knows that all men will always have logs in their eyes, never impartial enough to judge fairly. He cautioned us not to judge, lest we be judged.

Grace is all about cutting slack! If we aspire to graciousness, let's start by cutting one another more slack. If we were given the same harsh upbringing, mishaps, curve balls and disappointments, we would in all likelihood behave in the same twisted way as those we judge. Jesus is our example. He never once withheld healing from those who asked for it— nor did He pass judgement upon them, regardless of their sinfulness— always more than willing to forgive. If He didn't judge, then how dare we? Have you noticed that the only people Jesus had any harsh words for were religious people? Makes one think, doesn't it?

When Jesus cautioned us not to Judge, He was expressing His original desire and plan for mankind. If men and women hadn't acquired the knowledge of good and evil from eating the forbidden fruit, we would not have the poisonous knowledge that destroys treasured relationships, and more especially, destroys our cherished relationship with our precious heavenly Father.

The judgemental perspectives acquired from the fruit endowed Adam and Eve with a perspective of offense taking and strife, equipping them to inflict imperfect judgement upon their first victims, that being themselves! Self-recrimination made a dog's breakfast of what they thought of themselves.

In their shame they hid from God—another relationship trashed! A once beautiful divine romance, now in tatters, with many more casualties to follow. Cain, as self-appointed judge, executed his brother. Adam and

Eve's legacy of skewed judgement continues in our day and age to distort perspectives—dividing and destroying cherished friendships.

The consequences of man's imperfect judgements have escalated into terrorism of unimaginable proportions, maiming and destroying innocent men, women and children. All it takes is so-called righteous judgement in the hands of flawed individuals—imperfect individuals forced to exercise perfect judgement—not something they can achieve! It takes perfection to judge perfectly—something none of us possess. The one whose nickname is *"accuser of the brethren"* turns us into accusers of the brethren. Here's the dilemma—we cannot be accusers and lovers at the same time. God wants us to receive His love in order that we may pass it on. But for as long as we reserve the right to judge one another, it's simply not going to happen!

God's love is unconditional, and He wants us to pass it on in its unconditional form. Sadly, for as long as we reserve the right to be offended, love doesn't stand much chance of survival. Like oil and water, taking offense and giving love just don't mix! It has to be one or the other—never both! Judgement of a person muddies our love for that person. And insincere love is distasteful to the receiver. Unconditional love can only be practiced in "the absence of judgement"—a vacuum to be replaced with *"grace"*. In other words, we dare not hold onto our right to judge others. God's love is not called agape love for nothing!

Did Jesus say that his followers would be known for their dignity, religiosity, superiority or snobbery? No, He said that they would be known for their love. Sadly, Christians are often known for offence taking, aspersion casting and prejudice harbouring.

For instance, blasphemy: Believers are apt to take offence at the bad language of non-believers, and worse still, are not shy to tell them. "Please don't curse my best friend", they say. Their bad language doesn't offend God in the least bit. He's not trying to get them to change their language,

He's trying to gain a relationship with them, and that should be our aim too.

By expressing these forms of judgement, we don't endear ourselves; we alienate ourselves! In the past I have been guilty of taking blasphemers to task. None of these individuals ever changed the way they spoke when I wasn't around, but were careful to modify their speech in my presence, regularly apologising for slips of the tongue. My criticism played no part in changing them, it only served to build walls. Consequently, their position before God remains unchanged. We have simply added one more sin to their account—that of pretence.

I am not making a case for exposing ourselves to all manner of foul language and gutter talk. I am making a case for exposing the lost to all manner of unconditional love and acceptance. They simply cannot resist grace—nothing can be more overwhelming than to be loved without reason. Grace is merciful and forgiving, something immensely more impactful than judgement. Anything less does not possess the power to win friends and influence people.

Let's face it, God didn't win us over with judgement; He did it with mercy and grace! He desires that we extend to others the same measure of undeserved favour and grace that He extends to us.

God hears their bad language day in and day out while they are not pretending in our presence. How does He respond to it? By taking offence? "No, I came to save such as these. I went through the pain of the cruel cross for their sakes—I desperately desire their hearts". Their language is simply a product of their hearts. "Out of the abundance of the heart the mouth speaks. Hearts captured by love speak a different language."

Satan is pleased when we play the game by his rules. When we attempt to judge and love at the same time, we don't leave people with a lasting impression of our love; it's our judgement that lingers—a bitter taste and bad impression, not only of us, but also of our God. They get to thinking that He is just as unaccepting of them as we are. Sadly, they are often left with a warped impression of His gracious character. They never discover that they can approach Him just as they are. Given our offence taking, how will they ever feel comfortable with Him as an offence taker? They'll mistakenly feel that they need to shape up before they can turn to Him, and consequently never do. Let's be honest, we, like them, also sin. What could possibly be more discrediting of our witness than holier than thouness!

Satan's game is to get people to try to improve their behaviour in an effort to impress God. He knows they will fail—it is inevitable! And their failed attempts will take them down the slippery slope of shame, where a relationship with God will be even less likely!

God isn't one bit impressed with evil hearts pretending piety. We may be impressed with outward piousness, but not Him; He is concerned with what's going on in our hearts. But thankfully, once He has changed a heart, it no longer takes pleasure in unsavoury behaviour.

Satan doesn't want Christians to discover this, so he gets them to piously take offence at unbeliever's language. What are unbelievers to think? They don't see a loving Saviour; they only see His people misrepresenting His character. How can they be drawn to a loving Saviour while His children are driving a wedge between them and Him? Though we are forbidden to judge others, yet we continue to fall for the forbidden fruit, thereby following in Eve's murky footprints.

When Christians encounter spiritual darkness, their most powerful influence is not criticism; it is to shine their light of grace. There is only one light that a Christian should be giving off, and that is the bright light of empathy, unconditional love and acceptance—even to the worst of offenders. Jesus was the friend of prostitutes and crooks—He had no words of judgement for the woman caught in adultery.

We are not meant to shine the harsh light of judgement, exposing the weaknesses of others. We are to expose God's love and acceptance of them exactly as they are right now. Unbelievers don't see God; they only see His children. If His children are prejudiced and judgemental, guess what conclusions they reach concerning their Father? We can't blame them for thinking that He is every bit as prejudiced and judgemental as His holier than thou kids.

"Well, He is the great judge, isn't He?" That's what Satan would have us believe, but what does the Bible say? *"And the Father leaves all judgment to his Son"* (John 5:22). Our Father doesn't judge us, He gave that responsibility to Jesus. Now listen to what Jesus had to say about His role as our judge. *"I am not judging anyone"* (John 8:15). Neither God nor Jesus judges us. The truth is, *"God did not send his Son into the world to condemn it, but to save it"* (John 3:17). God refrains from judgement, until the end of the age. Jesus didn't use judgement to win the lost; He used unconditional love, mercy and grace! We are to emulate Him, showing nothing but unqualified love and acceptance regardless of a person's affability. Lovable or obnoxious, agape love remains agape love!

First prize for the most repulsive of all humanity would probably go to Jeffrey Dahmer. He enticed young men into his home where he would kill them, commit acts of necrophilia and then eat them. He destroyed sixteen young lives in their prime. Surely, He deserves to forfeit his life in exchange for the sixteen he took? But one life can never be payment enough for sixteen—it's an unfair exchange!

Police officers found the stench of death and rotting flesh to be overwhelming. Dismembered bodies, skulls and a human head sat on refrigerator shelves. The kitchen was covered with Polaroid photos of mutilated men.

Heads and human meat were in the freezer. Hands from several victims and a penis were in a pot. Two boiled skulls painted grey were on a bedroom closet shelf. Male genitalia were also found preserved in formaldehyde. There were hundreds of photos of victims before, during and after their gruesome murders. The sickening thought of the stench of decomposing corpses being sexually abused, mutilated and eaten, brought a morbid sense of revulsion upon the officers.

There was an altar of candles and human skulls in Dahmer's closet. He planned to create a shrine using skulls, other human trophies and a statue of a griffin to honour evil. He claimed that it gave him special powers and energies that helped him socially and financially.

On 17 February 1992 the court sentenced Dahmer to fifteen consecutive life sentences, a minimum of 936 years. On 16 May 1992 a consecutive life sentence was added for another 1978 murder. Sixteen young lives snuffed out to satisfy one maniac's warped desire to have sex with corpses.

Does this story nauseate and disgust you? Do you feel that a perpetrator of such base depravity deserves to burn in hell? Would it surprise you to know that that is not how God feels about Jeffrey Dahmer? Would you be surprised to know that while he was in the very act of tearing each victim limb from limb, cooking the flesh from the bone and devouring them that God's love for him never even skipped a beat? After the sixteenth murder, God still loved him as dearly as He had loved Him on the day he was born. While he was swallowing his last victim's heart, God didn't love him any less than He loves His beloved Son, Jesus. Jesus prayed to the Father, *"You love them as much as you love me"* (John 17:23). God the Father did not love Jesus one iota more than he loved this depraved maniac.

On 28 November 1994, Dahmer was murdered in prison by a fellow inmate. Dahmer thought nothing of stealing the innocent lives of young men, sentencing the ones who did not know Jesus as Saviour to the fires of Hell. Surely, he deserved nothing less than the blaze of Hades' flames?

You may be thinking, "What goes around comes around—good riddance! Hell is too good for him! Turn up the heat and let him fry for eternity!" But not God!

In reality, the moment he died, he was instantly transported into the loving arms of Jesus, and thereafter ushered to a magnificent mansion that he will forever occupy. God blotted out his sins. God doesn't even have any record of his depravity. In fact, He can't even remember that he sinned. *"I will forgive their iniquity, and I will remember their sin no more"* (Jer 31:34 KJV).

Just before he was murdered, Dahmer committed his life to Christ, and God instantly acquitted him of all his depravity. Doesn't such mercy just appal you? There is no justice in this! Surely there must be a limit to God's love—a breaking point? To be honest, this is where I lose it—to my peanut brain such depravity is unforgivable! I am confused by such graciousness! How dare God give him the same forgiveness He gave to the saintly mother Teresa whose worst sin may have been something as harmless as impatience? I have to admit that God's love is infinitely beyond my wildest imagination, far too much for my untheological mind to comprehend. For me to understand such infinite love is like trying to grasp the concept of the endlessness of space. It's way beyond my intelligence— far too mysterious to figure out.

Dahmer didn't even have enough time to mend his ways, but then again, God doesn't require this of us. Changing us is something He wants to do for us all by Himself. He does this by changing our hearts' desires little by little as we surrender little by little to His loving advances. He doesn't expect us to modify our behaviour. When we are constrained by His love, we find, to our surprise and delight, that we are behaving differently.

It is infinitely easier to surrender to love than to accusations and judgements. Being loved so unconditionally has a way of changing our ingrained desires—the allure of sin soon fades!

The good news is that we are not expected to change ourselves—that is something His love does—it changes us at heart level. It becomes a simple matter of living out what His love has inspired within us. It doesn't take long before, to our surprise and delight, we discover that we are behaving differently! When we turn our irksome ways over to Him, our desires undergo a love adjustment. With adjusted values, we don't need to be cajoled into shaping up—offensive behaviour simply loses its appeal!

When Adam and Eve ate the forbidden fruit of the knowledge of good and evil, it wasn't only judgement that they suddenly became aware of— it opened a door to new possibilities—they could achieve their dreams through treachery and deceit. *"For you are the children of your father the devil, and you love to do the evil things he does. He was a murderer from the beginning. He has always hated the truth, because there is no truth in him. When he lies, it is consistent with his character; for he is a liar and the father of lies"* (John 8:44). Before Satan deceived Adam and Eve, they never had to strive to not lie—the concept of lying had never even occurred to them.

All sin came into the world through deception, and it is deception that perpetuates sin. People are deceived into believing that a lie can bring them profit. A lying businessman may close a deal but will ultimately lose the respect of others! A cheating husband may be able to deceive his wife but ultimately lose the trust of his family!

The glitter of riches is Satan's lying lure. Like a fisherman's lure, attractive feathers promise the fish a tasty treat, but the feathers conceal a deadly hook. The unfortunate fish is persuaded to give up his life for nothing more than a mouthful of deception. The fisherman has no conscience as he fries the confused fish in a pan over a fire for breakfast.

Likewise, Satan has no conscience as he watches us squirm under the heat of the fire. He promises us happiness, and then we wonder why we're unhappy. In our pursuit of happiness, we may compromise virtuous values by lying our way to the top. People lie on their CVs to gain a job, and then wonder why they hate their jobs. Some lie and exaggerate to gain the respect of others, but only succeed in losing their trust.

None of Satan's promises are worth pursuing. Whatever we gain through deceit will ultimately come back to bite us. If we have gained something that is not ours, we will lose something that is ours. If we despise Satan for deceiving Eve, we should be equally despising of every temptation put our way. We should see it for what it is—dethroning, demoting, depressing, debasing, debilitating, defeating, defrauding, degrading, deluding, demeaning, demoralizing, denigrating, depleting, deposing, depreciating, depriving, derailing, disparaging, destituting, destroying, detouring, devastating, devoiding! A price too awful to contemplate! Why would we be willing to forfeit our treasured kingdom privileges and our treasured relationship with the only One who truly loves us—exchanging true life for empty promises?

That fateful day when Eve took the bait, not only did she and her husband lose their dominion, but so did all of their descendants. They were not promoted as Satan had promised; they were demoted—lost fellowship with their Father—relegated from kingly reign to labouring by the sweat of their brow—from painless childbirth to sheer agony. Is our memory really that short? Have we forgotten what it cost Eve? Can't we see disaster staring us in the face every time temptation comes knocking? Can we be so naive, taking the bait, knowing full well the pain that follows trysts with forbidden pleasures?

At enormous cost to Himself, Jesus regained Adam's lost dominion and now offers it to whomsoever will receive it. How is it that we are so eager to trade this amazing prize for a moment's pleasure? Why are we bothering with it? Have we forgotten the value we have in Christ?

If you have a portrait in your possession and don't know about the fame of the artist who painted it, you may accept a price far short of its true market value. Some have had portraits painted of themselves. No matter how good the artist's depiction in oils may be, it has little value, unless of course, the artist is famous. It is His fame that adds value to His artwork! Jesus is the artist and He has skilfully painted our portraits *"in Christ"*, making all the difference to our value! Despite this, many still sell themselves short—thoughtlessly trading the living works of art that they are, for nothing but the empty promises of the world. We need to rediscover the priceless value of our princely status so that we are not so easily cheated out of our divine royalty!

Knowledge that Entices

The knowledge of evil that dawned upon Adam and Eve after eating the forbidden fruit had another sad outcome. Evil opened up a whole plethora of new possibilities. Up till then, they had been blissfully unaware of a concept called "evil", but with this knowledge, they could achieve their goals by other means—devious means!

Also, their newly gained knowledge brought about an awareness of personal sinfulness, a concept that would damage their self-images, thus causing them to feel unworthy of God's affection. Before long, they were living up to the unfortunate images they had formed of themselves.

God had good reason for forbidding them from eating from this tree. He knew it would give them reason to adopt deception as an ally—a devious way to further their aims. So, it is not surprising that, after eating from it, they found themselves deceiving each other. As if that wasn't terrible enough, they took it a step further, attempting to deceive God. For the first time, they would experience guilt, something that would induce a sense of shame and unworthiness. That's all it took to ruin a perfect relationship!

God foreknew that, by giving Adam and Eve dominion over the earth, He was risking much. In order for dominion to be unfettered, it must include freedom of choice. They were free to choose to obey or to disobey!

Imagine, if Adam had chosen the tree of life rather than the forbidden tree. In doing so, he would have fed from the very life of God. Instead, he chose to exist on dented self-esteem, a self-defeating sin consciousness. Gone were the days when he could commune with God in the cool of the day without a flinch of embarrassment.

I think it is safe to say that each and every one of us can identify with him—we have all fallen short of the glory of God and felt the shame he felt. But what good can possibly come from shame? Self-debilitation and self-reproach, is that all it can produce?

God continues to give us the same choices He gave Adam. He cautions us not to eat from the tree of the Knowledge of Good and Evil. How sad to see so many choosing to ignore His warning. They do this by continuously bringing to mind their sinfulness, rather than their righteousness. Some go to church, week after week, just to be reminded of how sinful and deficient they are. They feast from the tree of the Knowledge of Good and Evil, when they should be indulging in the luscious fruit of the Tree of Life. What a crying shame! This should be the place where we are edified with the superlative abounding effervesce of God's life!

Two prisoners, John and Peter, were released from jail on the same day. Both were taken home by their fathers. John's father gave his son a dressing down, telling him that, because of his past record, he could not be trusted, and that he would be keeping a watch over him; while Peter's father told his son that all was forgiven and that, despite his shaky past, he loved him dearly and trusted him to make something worthwhile of his life.

What influence would these two contrasting attitudes have upon their sons? We might feel that a stern, untrusting confrontational approach would achieve deeper remorse and give a stronger reason for change, than a loving and trusting approach. The truth is that people live up to the image that is handed down to them. John is likely to find himself back in prison, as he lives up to the low opinion handed down to him by his untrusting father; while Peter is more likely to take a turn for the better as he endeavours to live up to his dad's high opinion of him.

And so, it is with our heavenly Father. He doesn't remind us of our sins, He reminds us of our righteousness in Christ Jesus. Like Peter's dad, He tells us how much He loves us; graciously wooing us with His affection—using kindness and acceptance to nurture and build our confidence in Him. The bottom line is that hurting people go out of their way to hurt people, while loved people go out of their way to love people!

To see ourselves in the way that our loving heavenly Father sees us, is to see ourselves as sons and daughters created in His image, accepted, even though we're hopelessly unable to live up to His perfect standard. Yet many choose to war against sin. To do this, they must ignore what was accomplished for them on the cross—the plain truth is that the battle is over—Jesus has overcome!

Though Jesus came to give us abundant life, many choose deficiency rather than abundance. Some think that poverty is pleasing to God.

How sad it is that so many churches feel duty bound to bully any hope of freedom out of their devotees. Hurting people go to these institutions seeking God's help. But instead of finding the liberty and abundant life Jesus promised, they come away as lesser human beings. Consigned to earning God's favour through modifying their actions; never getting to understand that God's favour is not for sale!

Striving for holiness is endless, life sapping and entirely futile. With failure after failure, we never get to feel worthy enough to be favoured. When expectation upon expectation is dashed, disenchantment soon sets in. When aspirations remain unfulfilled and hopes remain beyond our grasp, we tend to beat ourselves up with despondency. But, unbeknown to us, the *"abundant life"* we so eagerly seek is already entirely ours!

While we are intent upon eating the forbidden fruit, we miss out on God's good intentions for us. It's not our shortcomings, but our likeness to Him that we should be meditating upon. Afterall, isn't Jesus the prototype of every believer? Aren't our lives meant to be a carbon copy of His life? He didn't invest mere words in us; He invested Himself in us, wanting us to perform far greater miracles than He ever did!

As modern-day believers, what is it that gives us knowledge of good and evil? Is it not Old Covenant Law coupled with denominational legalism? How many of us are aware of how costly a little dabbling with the law can be? Believers are so easily disinherited! Sadly, few actually embrace the liberty for which Jesus paid so dearly on the cross. The more we eat of the law, the worse we feel about ourselves—making us ever less likely to experience intimacy with One who is perfect—shame just keeps getting in the way! Instead of going to the Tree of Life to discover our sinlessness *"in Christ"*, we go to the law, the tree of good and evil, to discredit ourselves.

Sadly, many see self-debasement as piety. How unfortunate! Jesus came to elevate believers—help them discover their divine similarity to Himself! Nothing could not be more obvious: He does not desire that we model ourselves on inferiority; He desires that we model ourselves on His perfection. He didn't come to lay blame; He came to liberate us from blame! He did not have demotion in mind; He had promotion in mind—elevating His children to the rank of princes and princesses in His glorious kingdom!

If we do not see it this way, we are likely to fall for religious debasement, making divine elevation and advancement even less likely. Just as we cannot be intimate with worms, our heavenly Father cannot be intimate with us when we make ourselves out to be less than what He has made us to be "in Himself". God desires a relationship with children, not worms!

How do believers compensate for lack of divine intimacy? Sadly, many turn to religious routines, a poor substitute!

When our good works don't measure up to religious expectations, we tend to beat ourselves to a pulp and promise to try even harder. Worse still, we are religiously persuaded to consider our poor self-images to be a mark of religious humility.

Religion has fooled us into accepting self-defacement, self-belittlement and self-denigration as marks of piety and saintliness. There are those who crawl on their knees up hundreds of cathedral stairs in an effort to prove their devotion to their Saviour. Aren't we doing exactly the same, though less obvious? We striving to impress God with our pious works and law keeping? When we fail to come up to scratch, we feel duty bound to come down hard on ourselves. Even though our very best efforts have never led to the intimacy we so dearly desire, we just keep soldiering on in hope of better outcomes.

Just as salvation cannot be attained through self-effort; so it is with intimacy—it can only be attained through accepting that we are in perfectly good standing, something for which we can take no credit—Jesus did it all!

It was Satan who convinced Eve that God could not be trusted. Up to then, everything Adam and Eve wanted was available to them without charge. But instead of the superior enlightenment promised by Satan, they were enlightened to their unworthiness. Despite doing all they could to remedy their predicament, going so far as to strive for something, that unbeknown to them, could not be attained, they pressed on regardless. Similarly, in our day and age, many are caught up in religiousness—doggedly using ritualistic meaninglessness to strive for divine acceptance.

Jesus came to reinstate His Father's original intention for mankind, came to re-establish favour without the help of religious striving.

Through the centuries, men and women have sought intimacy with God through self-debasement and poverty. Hundreds of monasteries scattered across the globe attest to mankind's self-debasing attempts to find God's approval. Each Monastery of Meteora in Greece is perched high atop of tall cliff faced finger like peaks, standing majestically over Greece's central plains.

Communities of monks live in seclusion on top of these enormous rocky spires, entirely cut off from society. Originally, the only access to these monasteries was by way of gantries. Monks were winched up sheer cliff faces to live in secluded isolation.

Through separation from society, in poverty, obedience to traditions and mental prayer, they strove for sinlessness—endeavouring to be in tune with God. With selfless discipline, they repressed their bodies and minds into spiritual submission.

Not content with this level of self-deprecation, some monks desiring an even higher level of God's acceptance, constructed scaffoldings secured halfway up these sheer rock faces. On these structures, in complete solitude, with no escape, they braved the harsh elements for extended periods, starving their bodies and minds of all pleasures in a quest to attain higher spirituality.

Before we judge such desperate attempts to attain intimacy with God, let us look at our own strivings. We don't have to be in a traditional church to be ritualistic. We may not view our spiritual routines in the same light as the self-effacing rituals of these monks, but if by our routines we are striving to make ourselves more acceptable to God, how are our efforts any different to theirs? Good spiritual exercises like prayer, praise, worship, thanksgiving, praying in the spirit, raising our hands to God, clapping, dancing before the Lord and fasting can be equally futile if done in the hope of gaining God's approval.

If we feel the need to do these things to make ourselves more acceptable to God, then we are saying that the blood of Jesus is deficient and in need of our help. If the blood of Jesus needs religious gymnastics to make it more effective than it already is, then we are in serious trouble. If, by our actions, we infer that the blood of Jesus is less veracious than the Bible claims it to be, we end up with less than the Bible promises. Perhaps it is time for us to examine our spiritual disciplines. Could they possibly be serving only to nullify the potency and purpose of the blood of Jesus in our lives.

Trying to fulfil the law can so easily become a substitute for intimacy with our Lord and Saviour. Satan has no problem with law keeping. He knows that striving will keep us side-tracked. Satan may lack integrity, but he certainly does not lack cunning. He is fully aware that intimacy with God cannot be obtained through personal right making. He also knows that law keeping makes faith useless, and Christ of no effect. *"For if you are trying to make yourselves right with God by keeping the law, you have been cut off from Christ! You have fallen away from God's grace"* (Gal 5:4).

Satan couldn't be happier seeing us going this route—a pathway to futility, a country mile from divine intimacy. He misuses the law to side-track God's good people from obtaining the ultimate gift, which in a word is *"grace"!* Trying to keep Old Testament law does nothing more than bring about a heightened consciousness of sin, which in turn leads to a heightened consciousness of unworthiness in the presence of a holy God.

We are free to choose either a life of lack or of abundance. Lack puts us into a mind-set of desperation, while abundance puts us into a mind-set of generosity. Our Father is beyond extravagant! He delights in lavishing favour upon His children! His generosity motivating our generosity!

When we partake of the forbidden fruit, which is the law, we partake of the lie that God cannot be trusted. The serpent put doubt in Eve's mind when he stated, *"Ye shall not surely die: For God doth know that in the day ye eat thereof, then your eyes shall be opened, and ye shall be as gods, knowing good and evil"* (Gen 3:4, 5 KJV). He failed to tell Eve that her knowledge of good and evil would get her and all her offspring into a whole heap of trouble. We are simply not equipped to use this knowledge wisely—we do not possess the perfection with which to make perfect judgements.

The lie that God could not be trusted, continues to be bought by believers to this very day. God says that He will supply all our needs according to His riches in Glory, but we say, "We cannot pay our bills." He says that by His stripes we were healed, but we say, "I am sick." He says that we are more than conquerors, but we say, "Circumstances are against us." He says that we can do all things through Christ, but we say, "I can't go on."

The lie causes us to doubt God, and that's enough to keep the miraculous out of our lives. For as long as we do not operate in our God given authority, circumstances will continue to have the last say over our happiness. What's the point of having authority over devils, if we can't even rule over circumstances?

Is God Guilty?

If we believe that God is in total control of running the world, we could conclude that He is not doing a very good job of it. You don't have to look too far. Our newspapers and TV news casts attest to the chaos: Terrorism, carjacking, armed robbery, rape and murder, not to mention natural disasters and accidents—obituary columns attest to a multitude of tragedies.

How often have we run to God's defence with all kinds of Christianese explanations, trying to convince those suffering that God knows what He is doing. We Say, "God's ways are higher than our ways," and, "It's for God to know and not for us to question." Then we tell them, "God does these things to us because He loves us." And so, we cover for God. Again, it's God who gets the blame.

We do this innocently. We believe Him to be in control and therefore responsible for both good and bad, so we feel compelled to help people to understand that He hurts them with the very best of intentions.

Answers to the following questions may give us a clearer perspective of who is responsible for all this chaos. If God is always in control:

- Does He really intend doing good to us through murder and rape?
- Does He cause tragedy to teach us lessons?

- If all things work together for good, is He causing tragedy in order to bless us?
- Does He really collaborate with Satan to teach us lessons?
- Does He use sickness to draw us closer to Him?
- Does he use the refiner's fire to shape our characters?

Let's look a little closer into each of these questions:

Does God really intend doing good to us through murder and rape?

If you wanted to discipline your child, would you ask a paedophile to help you do it? Of course not! Any rational person would regard such a notion as insanity. Don't you think God knows that too?

To assume that God conspires with evil to do good to us, is to admit that God is not entirely good. If He is not entirely good on one issue, then He cannot be trusted to keep His word on any other issue. In taking this line, how could we ever be sure of our salvation? If any part of the Bible is a myth, why should we believe any other part of it? It only takes one falsehood on God's part to bring the entire integrity of the Bible into question. But, if we accept the infallibility of the scriptures, we must accept what they have to say about Him. There is not an ounce of evil in Him, *"There is nothing but goodness in him!"* (Psalm 92:15).

Does God cause tragedy to teach us a lesson?

If we were to assume that God causes tragedy to teach us lessons, we would have to conclude that He is a sadist. As a small child, my mother chided me for catching flies trapped against the windowpane. I pulled their legs and wings off to see how well they would fare without them. You could say I was teaching flies a lesson in survival—helping them to rejoice in their hardship. How mindless is that?

Yes, God enables us to survive hardships, but should we be blaming Him for causing hardships? If we were to believe that God stoops to sadism, how could anybody possibly feel safe in His care? If He can be otherwise at times, how could we be sure that we'll find Him in a good mood? With our feebleness, would we even dare set foot in His presence? I don't think so! You may say that you deserve nothing more than a dressing down. Really? Then can you explain why He gave us grace? He paid an enormous price for it!

If all things work together for good, is He causing tragedy in order to bless us?

If all things work together for good, then we need to find out who is responsible for doing the things that God ultimately switches to our benefit. The word says, *"You intended to harm me, but God intended it all for good"* (Gen 50:20). From these words it would seem that we should be laying blame upon the enemy; not upon the Saviour! Obviously, it is somebody else's mess that God is able to turn to our benefit. Sometimes it's not even Satan, it's just plain and simply circumstances—being in the wrong place at the wrong time. Added to this, there are times when our stupidity gets us into all kinds of fixes.

Does God really collaborate with Satan to teach us lessons?

Satan, God's archenemy, was banished from God's presence. Never forget: God is altogether good, and Satan is altogether bad! God cannot look upon evil. Could you honestly imagine Him going into partnership with evil personified? If you were to start a new business, say a bank, what kind of partner would you choose to be in business with you? Someone you could trust with depositors' funds, or a bank robber out on parole? You may be thinking of Job as an exception to this rule. I have more to say about the book of Job at the end of this chapter.

Does God use sickness To draw us closer to Him?

Imagine for a moment that you wanted more of your son's affection. What would cause him to love you more? Would he be more inclined to love you if you put cancer on him, or if you lavished affection upon him? If you, being evil, would not stoop to putting cancer on your child, how much more a holy God? If you really believe that God puts cancer on you, then you had better not pray for healing. If cancer is God's will for you, then praying for healing would be defying His will!

What about medicine? If cancer is God's will for you, how dare you defy Him by trying to get better? If that were so, medicine, Chemo and Radium would all work against His will. Fortunately, it's not in His nature to put sickness onto His kids. To the contrary, He hates sickness so much that He took our sicknesses upon Himself, for by His stripes we were healed.

Does God use the refiner's fire to shape our characters?

"But who will be able to endure it when He comes? Who will be able to stand and face Him when He appears? For He will be like a blazing fire that refines metal, or like a strong soap that bleaches clothes. He will sit like a refiner of silver, burning away the dross. He will purify the Levites, refining them like gold and silver, so that they may once again offer acceptable sacrifices to the LORD" (Mal 3:2-3).

We are promised a process of refining by fire. In this scripture, God is the refiner. Even issues of our own making can be used by Him to refine our characters. We have a choice either to go about life our way or God's way. We often choose badly and end up suffering detrimental consequences. We may even have allowed sin to escalate to the point of giving Satan a stronghold in our lives. When we surrender an issue that has enslaved us, the intensity of its lure is extinguished. All it takes is obedience and an unwavering belief that God is entirely good!

"When you go through deep waters, I will be with you. When you go through rivers of difficulty, you will not drown. When you walk through the fire of oppression, you will not be burned up; the flames will not

consume you" (Isa 43:2). God promises that when we go through tribulations, the flames will not consume us. He has set a limit!

The three Hebrew boys had been arrested and brought before King Nebuchadnezzar for not obeying his decree to bow to the ground and worship the golden image of himself. The punishment for defying his decree was death by fiery furnace. Shadrach, Meshach, and Abednego replied, *"O Nebuchadnezzar, we do not need to defend ourselves before you. If we are thrown into the blazing furnace, the God whom we serve is able to save us. He will rescue us from your power, Your Majesty. But even if He doesn't, we want to make it clear to you, Your Majesty, that we will never serve your gods or worship the gold statue you have set up"* (Dan 3:16-18).

Infuriated by such bold-faced insolence, the king ordered that the fire be heated seven times hotter than usual. The king's strongest men bound them and cast them into the fire. As robust as the king's strongest men were, they were instantly killed by the intense heat of the blazing furnace.

Compare this scary trial with the trial that you are going through right now. Doesn't it pale by comparison? Of Course, while in the thick of it, nobody ever feels that their trial is trivial.

Suddenly, Nebuchadnezzar jumped up in amazement and exclaimed to his advisers, *"Didn't we tie up three men and throw them into the furnace?"* *"Yes, Your Majesty, we certainly did,"* they replied. *"Look!"* Nebuchadnezzar shouted. *"I see four men, unbound, walking around in the fire unharmed! And the fourth looks like a god!"* (Dan 3:24,25).

When we are persecuted for our faith, we can be sure that we will not have to endure the flames alone. As with the three Hebrew boys, God joins us in our ordeal. As you look around, things could not be bleaker. You feel hopeless and alone, but with spiritual eyes of faith, you find ample reason to take heart—standing beside you is One who is of infinite greatness. It might be exceedingly overwhelming to you, but certainly not to the greater One beside you. Nothing could ever be too difficult for the two of you to confront with aplomb!

"Then the high officers, officials, governors, and advisers crowded around them and saw that the fire had not touched them. Not a hair on their heads was singed, and their clothing was not scorched. They didn't even smell of smoke!" (Dan 3:27).

The absolute terror of the moment eventually subsides, and you realize that your trial has left you unscathed, but significantly stronger in faith.

How did the Hebrew boys benefit from such a terrifying ordeal? Benefit? Surely not? They were frightened out of their wits! I don't think so! Before the ordeal, they spoke with absolute confidence and trust in their God. After experiencing such a mighty victory, can you imagine what the ordeal did for their faith? What could be worse than the furnace? Criticism? Lack? Sickness? I don't think so! It would take a lot more than that to scare them. Clearly, anything else that life could throw at them would be trivial compared to the terror they had faced in the fiery furnace!

God is using life's experiences to develop our faith. Nothing is more important to Him than to be trusted by His children. Wavering faith expresses mistrust, and nobody enjoys being mistrusted, least of all God! In His estimation, faith counts for more than anything else. He values faith so highly that He counted Abraham's faith as righteousness. Praise God! Trials don't bring us down; they reinforce our confidence in God!

A women's group was doing a study of the book of Malachi. In chapter three, they came across a verse: *"He will sit as a refiner and purifier of silver."* This verse puzzled them. They wondered what they could learn of the character and nature of God in these words.

One of the women offered to find out about the process of refining silver and to inform the group at their next Bible Study. That week, she called up a silversmith and made an appointment to watch him at work.

She mentioned nothing about the reason for her interest; just that she was curious about the process of refining silver. As she watched, the silversmith held a large ladle of silver over the fire and let it heat up. He explained that in the refining of silver, one needed to hold the silver in the middle of the fire where the flames were at their fiercest so as to burn away the impurities.

That brought to mind the verse, *"He sits as a refiner and purifier of silver."* Maybe God needs to hold us over the heat.

She asked the silversmith if it was true that he had to sit in front of the fire the whole time the silver was being refined. He nodded yes. He not only had to sit there holding it, but could not take his eyes off it for a moment. If the silver was left a moment too long in the flames, it would be destroyed.

After a moments silence, she asked, "How do you know when the silver is fully refined?" He smiled at her and answered, "Oh, that's easy—when I see my image reflected in it."

If today you are feeling the heat of the fire, remember that God has His eye on you, and will keep watching you, using just enough fire, making sure that you are not destroyed in the process. He knows that the moment He sees His image reflected in you, the process is complete! That's when you begin to look just like Him—a child of God, loving, confident, fearless and destined for victory!

Sometimes close relationships can rub us up the wrong way. We may become irritated with a person and wish to end the relationship—at times hoping never to meet the offensive individual again. What if God arranged the offensive relationship for our benefit? This may be the fire that God is using to bring our dross to the surface, so that we can surrender our personal impurities to the divine Refiner. We ought to welcome the fire, for without it, we remain murky, un-christlike, selfish and unattractive.

Origin of Evil

We cannot blame God for the origin of evil. It is not He who initiates it, it is we—it happens when we resist His good plans for us. Imagine how aggrieved He must feel when He calls us and we dig in our heels to go our own way! When we resist Him, it is His gracious plans to do us good that we are resisting—plans to give us a hope and a future; not an injury and a disaster. Each of the Old Testament prophets had much to say about God's dismay at His people's blatant disregard of His plans to bless them.

"What sorrow awaits My rebellious children," says the LORD. "You make plans that are contrary to Mine. You make alliances not directed by My Spirit, thus piling up your sins" (Isa 30:1).

God could not be held responsible for their flawed plans; they were totally contrary to His plans. In their rebellion, they were effectively saying that their plans were better than God's. In reality, what they were rejecting was an opportunity to participate in His glorious favour.

"O Jerusalem, Jerusalem, the city that kills the prophets and stones God's messengers! How often I have wanted to gather your children together as a hen protects her chicks beneath her wings, but you wouldn't let Me" (Mat 23:37).

Jesus was dismayed by His people's resistance to His desire to bless them. In rejecting His love, they effectively volunteered to remain guilty for their misdemeanours. They should not be blaming God for their tragedy. He is by no means guilty!

The Flawed Theology of Job

The connection between divine punishment and suffering is only mentioned in the Bible as a flat-out denial that any such a connection exists.

Though Job's friends blamed God for Job's afflictions, the whole point of the book of Job is to expose their ignorance of God's gracious character.

Satan is not an agent of God, rather he roams to and fro, looking for opportunities to wreak havoc. How did Satan get permission to wreak havoc upon Job? It was his fear that gave Satan permission! Job was protected by a hedge of faith, which shielded him from Satan's trickery. But his fear brought about a gap in his hedge, and this allowed Satan to sneak in.

Isn't it interesting that at the end of the book of Job, the Lord disagrees with Job and his friends' theology, and that Job repents for blaming God? It was not God's will that was revealed in Job's afflictions; it was Satan's will.

Again, God is not to blame!

The Eco System

Weather patterns have changed. More storms and droughts than ever before. Extreme weather becoming ever more extreme. Hot days are hotter and cold days, colder. Is this God's sovereign interference, or are these patterns natural knock-on effects? Too much fossil fuel pollution causing a greenhouse effect, causing el Nino ocean warming, causing high pressure zones, causing winds to rush from high pressure zones to low pressure zones, causing storms in certain regions and droughts in others. One continent's troubled weather disturbing another continent's weather, and so the butterfly effect makes its way around the world—knock-ons upon knock-ons…

When God handed over the planet to man, it was in perfect equilibrium. But it didn't take too long for man's mismanagement to throw it off kilter. When people are drowned and homes destroyed by freak storms, is it God's fault, or are we simply reaping the consequences of our mismanagement?

Years of interference and misuse of natural resources have upset weather patterns. Ecological tampering: The deforestation of South America (the lungs of the earth); excessive fossil fuel pollution in China and the USA. Even something as insignificant as the CFCs from deodorant sprays have damaged the UV shield of our planet. Our desire to smell good caused a hole in the ozone layer, resulting in an epidemic of skin cancer. Various interferences, resulting in chaotic outcomes. One thing is certain, it is not God's fault!

We often hear TV reporters calling natural disasters Acts of God. How wrong can they be? Mankind is simply reaping what mankind has sown. Humanity's misguided wisdom and greed is way out of sync with God's delicately balanced ecology. Poor choices have left us to contend with a legacy of chaos!

Although God is not responsible for the knock-ons, it doesn't mean that God can't suspend nature. It's just that He has chosen to wait for our faith declarations before stepping in. He honours the dominion He conferred upon to us. *"Ask the Lord for rain in the spring and He will give it"* (Zec 10:1). He is ready to interrupt the natural with the supernatural, but He doesn't move uninvited—He respects the dominion He granted us. As dominion holders, He has left us with the choice of either to invite His intervention or to go it alone!

More than a century ago, winds were responsible for shifting sand dunes to the point of encroaching upon some South African seaside cities. Sand was blowing in faster than it could be cleared. Local authorities had to come up with a better plan. They decided to plant vegetation on the dunes to bind the sand and prevent further encroachment. The problem was that our indigenous plants could not survive in sand. Hardier vegetation was needed.

At last the problem was dealt with by importing desert vegetation from Australia. At first, it seemed to solve the problem! But what the City fathers did not foresee, was that foreign invasive vegetation would lead to problems, far greater than the nuisance of the dunes. The proliferation of the vegetation didn't stop at the dunes' edge, it surged ahead, invading good farmland. Farmers were losing valuable land to invasive vegetation far faster than they could cut it back. As years passed, the problem compounded. Is God to blame? After all, wasn't it He who created the vegetation in the first place?

But then again, was it He who came up with this hairbrained idea? The eco system He established was perfectly well balanced before mankind upset it. God, being holy, couldn't take back control just because mankind messed up. As much as He may have wanted to, He was too honourable for that! He honours the sovereign will He gave us. We are free to exercise dominion as we see fit. He even honours our right to mess up. If we mismanage the Earth, we must live with the consequences of our mismanagement.

The same goes for our personal lives. Can we blame God for the outcome of our poor choices? Can young teenagers blame God for getting them pregnant, can smokers blame God for their lung cancer, can alcoholics blame Him for cirrhosis of the liver?

But here's the good news: We cannot mess up our lives beyond God's ability to fix. He requires no more than an invitation!

Reaping What We Sow

God initiated the principle of seedtime and harvest. When we plant bean seed, we get beans, and when we plant carrot seed, we get carrots. We will never reap beans from carrot seed. When we plant judgement, we reap the judgement of others. When we spread hatred, we reap the hatred of others. Let's not kid ourselves: Sin comes back to bite us, in the same way that kindness comes back to enrich us! We reap what we sow!

When we reap disappointment from our own negligence, we can't blame God saying, "He is trying to teach us something." We must take responsibility for our actions. For every action there is a reaction—not necessarily a God reaction—a seedtime and harvest reaction. Despite this, many have the gall to blame God!

Satan's Strategy

Satan doesn't like anybody at all, not even those who place their trust in him. Satan hates Satanists. He promises them power, but only for the purposes of entrapment. Once they're in his evil clutches, he twists their minds—usurping their God ordained authority. In this way, he empowers himself. He does it by usurping them of their dominion, thereby gaining the right to accomplish his diabolical agenda of stealing and destroying.

If Satan cannot be trusted by his closest allies, how much less by his sworn enemies. As children of God, we represent his arch enemy and therefore bear the brunt of his attacks. Like a cheetah chasing a gazelle, he goes for the weakest in the herd. He cannot touch our heavenly Father, so he goes for His children, starting with the weakest in the herd—those lacking knowledge of their good standing with God—taking them out at will. But we are certainly not helpless. We bear lethal weapons of spiritual warfare—well able to overpower him!

Jesus' name in our mouths is enough to scares the living daylights out of Satan. He cannot withstand the word of our testimony. He has no answer for the blood of the Lamb—it renders him weak and ineffective. It takes God's word in our mouths to put him in his place, beneath our feet where he belongs!

Heavenly reinforcements are dispatched in response to our prayers— archangels and their hosts come to our rescue. Praise empowers them to do battle on our behalf against Satan's hordes. Steadfast faith makes us invincible in the face of satanic onslaught. He has been beaten by our elder brother, Jesus—rendered useless! Now all he can do is attempt to scare us into handing over our God-given authority!

"He saw a woman who had been crippled by an evil spirit. She had been bent double for eighteen years and was unable to stand up straight" (Luke 13:11). Please note, she was crippled by an evil spirit, one of Satan's mob, not God's. Her condition wasn't God's will, it was Satan's will. It wasn't, "God trying to teach her a lesson in patience or endurance," or some other trite Christianese cliché that Christians dish out in an effort to make sense of confusion. Every time Christians do this, they inadvertently let Satan off the hook, and unintentionally malign God's holy reputation.

How is it that those who love God the most are often the very ones to blame Him the most? We may cloak our accusations of Him in religious platitudes, which on the surface sound pious enough. But these well-used Christianese clichés are mostly nonsense, inspired by Satan to cast aspersions upon God's impeccable character, thus confusing Christians. He is hell bent on besmirching God's reputation; doing anything to bring His trustworthiness into question.

We can understand immature believers misunderstanding God to be the author of these awful deeds—they have been led to believe that He does it for their ultimate good. But how do we explain mature believers falling for this lie? Could it be that they feel the need to come up with a plausible explanation as to why their prayers don't get answered? I guess that some may have adopted the complacency of their Bible teachers, who tragically, can barely remember a prayer been answered. Sadly, the complacency of leadership soon becomes the complacency of followers. But the apathy of our mentors does not make apathy okay.

"And his disciples asked him, saying, Master, who did sin, this man, or his parents, that he was born blind. Jesus answered, Neither hath this man sinned, nor his parents: but that the works of God should be made manifest in him" (John 9:2,3).

In this story you might conclude that God put blindness on the man so that the works of God could be manifested in him. If that were so, this man lived a whole lifetime in utter darkness, an outcast of society, dependant on others, robbed of the joy of a normal childhood, just to give God a moment of glory. If this was true, then God isn't the loving Father we have been led to believe Him to be.

Surely, we know Jesus better than that? And because the Father is perfectly reflected in the life of Jesus, we also know the Father better than that. Could you imagine an earthly dad searing out the eyes of his infant child with a burning stick? How despicable would that be? If this view is totally inconsistent with imperfect earthly dads, how can we even begin to imagine this of our perfect heavenly Father? This is not what Jesus is saying here. I believe He is saying that it is not necessary to analyse the reasons for the problem. We have the power to fix it—let's get on with it! He wants us to demonstrate grace to the hurting, not by exposing their shame, but by covering their shame. Let's get on with it and perform the miraculous! If there are issues needing godly adjustment, the word tells us, *"The goodness of God leadeth thee to repentance"* (Rom 2:4 KJV). First the healing (*the goodness of God*), and then moral adjustment (*repentance*). It is vital to understand the sequence.

In the original Greek, John 9:3 doesn't say that the man was born blind so that the works of God might be revealed in him. It says let the works of God be revealed in him.

Christians often wrestle with these questions:

"Is God putting me through this trial to teach me something?"

"Is Satan up to his old tricks?"

"Am I reaping what I have sown?" And so on ad nauseam. So what? What does it matter? No matter who is responsible, all that is important is that we praise God regardless. He desperately wants to intervene—to switch the catastrophe that Satan intended for our harm into a wonderful benefit. But He cannot intervene without our permission. Worrying gives our enemy permission to wreak havoc; while praise, prayer and declaring our faith gives God permission to grant victory!

Did the people in the World Trade Centre Towers die because they had sinned? What about the 300 firemen who so selflessly ran into the towers to save perishing souls? There can be no motive purer than laying one's life down for another. Did they also perish for their sins?

Jesus dealt with this question 2000 years ago. Another tower had fallen, killing eighteen people. Jesus asked the question, *"Those eighteen, upon whom the tower in Siloam fell, and slew them, think ye that they were sinners above all men that dwelt in Jerusalem?"* Then He answered His own question, *"I tell you, nay..."* (Luke 13:4,5 KJV). Here Jesus puts to rest any such speculation about their deaths. They did not die for their sins. It is abundantly clear from Jesus' explanation of the tower of Siloam that the people who died on 9/11 did not die for their sins. Sometimes good people are in the wrong place at the wrong time.

An American friend of mine was traumatised at the thought of losing fellow Americans in the 9/11 tragedy. It pained him to think that so many had slipped into a Christ-less eternity. He poured the anguish of his heart out to the Lord, pleading for some explanation. Then he heard from the Lord. The Lord assured him that many had called on His name in time to be saved. He took comfort from this.

Later, one of the few survivors, an Assembly of God minister, told an amazing story. He had run down the stairs and gathered with many hundreds of people in the foyer of the second tower. Outside, light was all but blocked out—air thick with dust, smoke and debris from the first tower's collapse. The crowd within was in two minds: Do they take their chances and run out into the heavily laden murky air, or do they wait in the shelter of the foyer for the dust to settle? They had no way of knowing that the tower they were taking refuge in, was about to pancake down upon them.

In panic, many were screaming, "What must we do?" The minister shouted at the top of his voice, "Call on the name of Jesus!" There was one almighty response as their shout went up, "JESUS!" In the same instant, the tower fell upon them with a thunderous crash. This huge crowd instantly swept into the loving arms of their Saviour—for many a saviour they had never known. One moment sinners, the next, saints. Doesn't the Word tell us that those who call upon the name of the Lord would be saved? (Acts 2:21)

God didn't poison the minds of the terrorists to cause them to perform such a dastard deed. Satan was at work! But God was able to turn what was intended for their ill to benefit them. Not all were saved, salvation only went to those who called on His name. Wasn't this unfair? Couldn't God have made an exception and saved the others? If He had, He would have violated His word, and we all know that He would never do such a thing. He will always honour, even defend our right to choose hell in preference to heaven.

War in the Heavenlies

If God didn't cause the chaos, why are innocent children ending up molested, sick and dead? Our little Emma could not have done anything before her birth to deserve deafness, and what heinous sin could a seven-year-old have possibly done to deserve leukaemia? How do we explain the millions of promising young men and women's lives cut short in their prime by the wars of past ages? Why do bad things happen to good people?

"But the prince of the kingdom of Persia withstood me one and twenty days: but, lo, Michael, one of the chief princes, came to help me; and I remained there with the kings of Persia." (Dan 10:13 KJV). This is the angel's explanation as to why it took twenty-one days for Daniel to receive the answer to his prayer. He described a war in the heavenlies that prevented him from reaching Daniel sooner. In fact, the tide of the war was going against the angel of the Lord, and he needed help from someone stronger than himself. That's when Michael, the archangel came to his aid.

But surely God can do what He likes. How does Satan get to prevent Almighty God from carrying out His will? Do not lose sight of the fact that dominion of this Planet is in man's hands, not God's. God does not operate in man's dominion except by invitation. When He dispatches an answer to our prayers, it remains our responsibility to ensure that the angel's mission is accomplished. We need to stand against the powers and principalities that would prevent the angel from delivering his parcel. It takes prayers and declarations of unshakeable faith, together with praises and thanksgiving to open the way for miracles to reach us.

Often, when answers to our prayers are not immediately forthcoming, we conclude that it is not God's will to answer our prayers. In Daniel's case, he didn't come to this conclusion, he simply pressed on believing against all odds, until the angel broke through the powers and principalities. If he had concluded that it wasn't God's will and stopped believing, the angel would have lost the battle and Daniel would not have received the answer to his prayer.

This is happening every day. Angels lose the fight due to people giving up on their dreams. They simply rationalise that it is not God's will. Angels look to us to empower them in the fray. What happens in practice is that angels retreat in battle for lack of prayer support. They limp out of the war, battered and bruised as we fail to ensure their safe passage.

How long should we persist with confident expectation? As long as it takes! Of course, if delivery was dispatched at the precise moment of our first prayer, then subsequent praying should not take the form of asking—an additional delivery is not needed; it's the first delivery that's outstanding. It's not about pleading; it's about gratefully receiving by faith. Praise and thanksgiving release the faith that empowers angels to get the delivery to us.

How often does God get maligned by us; not because He let us down, but because we gave up on our dreams? We rationalise, saying that it wasn't His will in the first place? But in reality, He may have granted the answer to our request, but delivery failed to reach us because we failed to continue steadfastly in faith. His messengers need all the help they can get. Let's stand in unwavering faith!

Sovereignty

In case you have reserved the word Sovereignty exclusively to describe God's independent authority; bear in mind that it is also a word in common usage to describe earthly kingdoms and governments. It infers that governing bodies are independent. They have the right to decide for themselves without interference from outside sources—having authority to make and enforce their own laws. South Africa is a sovereign state, and Queen Elizabeth is the British Sovereign. Neither South Africa nor Britain need the United Nations to approve their laws—sovereignty allows them to decide for themselves.

God gave us a sovereign will—in other words, a free will allowing us to independently make our own decisions and then to live by their consequences, whether good or bad.

We know that God is sovereign. As such He can sovereignly decide to do anything, even to devolve sovereign responsibility on whomever He wishes. Once sovereignty has been conferred upon anybody, it can never be retracted, otherwise sovereignty is not sovereignty.

A free choice is not a free choice if the conferrer reserves the right to override free choices. In other words, when Adam was given dominion of the earth, he was also given the freedom to use or abuse his charge. If God had reserved the right to retract dominion, then we could say that Adam never actually had ownership and dominion in the first place.

In common law, upon transferring dominion of a property to another, the conferrer ceases to have a controlling interest in the property—leaving the conferee with the freedom to use his dominion in any way he may wish. He has every right to use it or abuse it. The conferrer has forfeited His right to interfere. And so it is with God. He created the earth and then put it in the hands of mankind. He has sovereignly chosen not to interfere, no matter how flawed mankind's management of it may be.

So, when Satan tricked Adam out of his dominion, God, as much as He may have wanted to, He could not interfere. When He gave a legal right to man to reign over this earth, He bound himself to abide by the legality of man's dominion. Though God had the ability to overcome Satan and restore Adam in a flash, He no longer had the legal right to do so. It was no longer within His jurisdiction. His righteous principles guarantee that He will always honour His word, and His word guarantees that He will not meddle with man's sovereign dominion.

If God has no right to interfere with our dominion, does Satan have a right to do so? Absolutely not! Unlike God, Satan is dishonourable and cannot be trusted. He will attempt to usurp our dominion, using deceit to defraud us of it. He doesn't miss a trick in the book, in fact, he wrote the filthy book! The trick he played on Eve continues to be played out on us, her descendants, and sadly, many fall for his lies. He never plays fair. He does all he can to get us to doubt the truth of God's words. Without question, mankind is more apt to doubt than to believe. Doubt is every bit as powerful as faith—it's a belief in the possibility of an undesirable outcome—trust in reverse—a conviction that God may not come through for us. That's all it takes to open the door to Satan—he takes every opportunity to administer disaster.

Wavering words of doubt and unbelief empower Satan, giving him permission to hijack our dominion and wreak havoc in our lives. When we give him or his demons an inch, they take the whole tape measure. They know that dominion can only be exercised on earth by those who have earthly bodies like Adam's, so they do all they can to establish strongholds within his descendants. Strongholds allow demons to assume a person's dominion, thereby empowering themselves to use that person's right of dominion for their own evil ends. If they can establish a stronghold in a life, they can destroy that person's happiness, joy, health, finances and relationships.

Many insist that only God has sovereignty over the Earth. But if that was so, they would have to explain why it is in such a mess. If this is the best He can do, then we would have to admit that He is not at all good at it—in fact, He has messed up big time!

Seeing that God is perfect in every respect, He is simply incapable of doing anything less than perfect. With all the abuse of power, corruption, wars, murders, rapes, molestations etc, it should be obvious that He is not sovereign over such hellish chaos. If God would never, no, could never, be a party to murder and rape, then someone else is obviously exercising his sovereign right. Blame God for our woes if you will. But what we choose to believe does not change the fact that God is perfect, incapable of error, or of any kind of wrongdoing. He is simply not to blame!

Unbelievers often use the chaos around them as an excuse to not believe in Jesus. They blame God for such things as the death of a loved one at the hands of a drunken driver. Well, God didn't tell the driver to drink himself into a stupor of irresponsibility and then instruct him to get behind the wheel and drive over somebody. Man has a sovereign right to choose to do good or evil. God doesn't remove that right. It was divinely bestowed upon mankind, and therefore, though God is sovereign, He has no legal right to stop people from sinning. Clearly, if He had retained this right, He would not have allowed Hitler to exterminate six million Jews!

With cunning and deceit, Satan tricks people into doubting that their prayers will be answered. He does this by reminding them of their sinfulness. Unfortunately, He is so crafty that he has no compunction when it comes to influencing good honest clergymen to derail the prayers of their followers. If he can get them to tell their flocks that their prayers cannot be answered while there is sin in their lives, their prayers will not get answered, and Satan will win the day! Clergymen do this in all sincerity with the very best of intentions. They forget that Jesus handled such issues very differently—never once making repentance a precondition for healing.

Unfortunately, such a notion causes their flocks to be more conscious of their sin than of their righteousness in Christ. By giving people a sinful image of themselves, they are likely to live up to that image, thus leading to even more sin. *"...the law gives sin its power"* (1Co 15:56).

God didn't give us a sinful image of ourselves. In saying that we are the righteousness of God in Christ, we were given a righteous image to live up to. Sure, we all know that our day to day lives are less than perfect.

Although sanctification is instantaneous, its process of revolutionising our behaviour is not—it is ongoing! If it was within our power to eradicate sin from our lives, and we were required to do this in order to have our prayers answered, then the continuing process of sanctification would serve no purpose. Although sanctification happened in a flash, yet it takes more than a lifetime to filter into our actions. Most of us have been around the block enough times to know that no-one, including the most pious of church leaders, have attained perfection.

I have seen church leaders' hearts exposed (including mine) during serious challenges, such as church splits. I have seen the worst come out of the best of us. Believe me, so-called mature Christians are far from perfect.

All men, at any stage of maturity in Christ, are still exceedingly evil when compared to Christ. We will never have our prayers answered if it must depend on our practical perfection. Thank God, Jesus never made sinlessness a condition for prayers to be answered, and neither should we.

Because we have a sovereign will, we often find ourselves at odds with God's sovereign will. This is not at all clever! To be at odds with God is to forfeit His wisdom, provision, healing and favour. When we choose to go our way, we reduce our divine effectiveness to the limitations of our human ineffectiveness. If we have chosen to live under our circumstances, we have chosen to be dominated by them. Is there any wonder that there is so much discontent going around? Of course, all of this can be avoided! God's way can be trusted to bring about the most favourable of outcomes to the most chaotic of circumstances.

When we choose to place our dominion under God's sovereignty, His resources are at our disposal. When we do this, we are no longer facing the world alone. We have a loving Father with a household of servants ready to do His bidding for us. Let's face it, having the guidance of the One who sees the future before it happens, we have an unfair advantage!

When we discover that our Father accepts us exactly as we are, we no longer need public approval. There is no need for name dropping and posturing to gain the approval of others. We are able to put down our guard and become vulnerable. Grace is about giving love and acceptance to people who don't deserve it, even going so far as to give to those who are most unlikely to return it. We choose not to be offended by obnoxiousness, accepting one another's shortcomings in the same way that Jesus accepts ours. Our desire to be loved is fulfilled in God's love for us. We draw from His resources—they're ours by inheritance.

A friend told me how he rescued a drowning woman in the surf. She was fighting to stay afloat, taking in much water, arms flailing in a wild panic, fighting her rescuer, pushing him under. He did his best to remain composed while trying to calm her. The only way he could pull her out of her panic was to give her a firm smack in the face. He was prepared to knock her out if necessary. One smack was all it took to get her to yield. Only once she had completely relaxed, was he able to swim her to the safety of the shore.

If we choose to stubbornly do our own thing our way, we will drown in the panic of trying to stay afloat in the turbulence of life's challenges. While we are doing it our way, God has to stand back and watch us drown. It is only when we yield and allow Him to have His way in our lives that He can rescue us. If we want the benefits of the Kingdom, we need to be under the government of the Kingdom, allowing Him to have His sovereign way in our lives.

A Monarch takes care of everybody within his or her kingdom but has no responsibility toward anybody outside of his or her domain. How do Christians put themselves beyond the domain of the Kingdom of God? Frank Sinatra gave us a clue in his arrogant song, "I did it my way". It's okay to do it our way, but the outcome of our doings will be at our expense—we'll forego our kingdom privileges. What a crying shame! Pride can be awfully costly!

Does God always get His Way?

The cross makes nonsense of the view that God's omnipotence equals getting His way all the time. Why would He have bled and died, except for a world that was not running true to His will?

Though He is omnipotent, He did not use His omnipotence to force us to love Him. He used self-sacrificial love to convince us of His noble intentions—going all the way to the cruellest punishment of all to prove His love for us. Doesn't the cross provide the most indisputable proof of all that He chose love rather than omnipotence to win our affections. With His omnipotence, He could have used brute force to strong arm us into a relationship. But not our God! He would never use his omnipotence to force us into anything. The cross, more than anything else, proves beyond any shadow of doubt that God is not responsible for bringing hardship and sickness upon us. The cross provides indisputable proof of grace of the most extreme kind. It reveals a God who is decidedly against every imaginable burden and sickness. If He chose to take the blame for each and every one of our failures, then without question, He deserves to be punished in the most excruciating way possible. If we are guilty, then He is guilty by choice, and deserves to be seriously taken out—massacred until there isn't a drop more of His blood to be let. With the most unimaginable cruelty, He must be tortured and killed for rape, murder, lying, hatred, offence taking and every falsehood—He is guilty as charged by choice!

After witnessing this most unselfish act of all, where does that leave us? Having read the Gospels, we are witnesses of the most surpassingly unimaginable extreme act of sacrificial love. Why? Why? Why? Why would anybody do this for a bunch of scally wags who are forever going to disappoint Him. Surely, the cross provides adequate proof that any sickness or hardship we may be experiencing, is certainly not from Him. How could He make it any clearer that He is not to blame?

That we will go through many troubles, is a given. The point is that God does not put them on us. He said, *"The righteous person faces many troubles, but the LORD comes to the rescue each time"* (Psalm 34:19 KJV). He is not in the business of putting hardships on us; He is in the business of rescuing us from hardships!

So many believe that God is in charge of the earth, therefore His will is always done. This view allows them to find an explanation as to why things go wrong. "God is trying to speak to you," they say, "He is drawing you nearer." So many explanations. But that is not what the Bible teaches. He simply cannot do His will on earth without the permission of mere mortals—He has vested dominion upon them. If He could do His will whenever He wanted, He wouldn't have instructed us to pray, *"Thy will be done in earth, as it is in heaven"* (Mat 6:10). If God desires to do His will on earth, why doesn't He just go ahead and do it? The answer is plain. He can't! This verse makes it clear—He needs our invitation.

How do we know that His will is not always done on earth? The whole reason for Jesus dying on the cross was because He wanted to establish His will in our lives. Without the cross, mankind would forever continue to run out of sync with His gracious plan for us. Do you really think God would have allowed His son to go through the pain and rejection of the cross if His will on earth was being fulfilled? Let's face it, both unbelievers and believers alike continue to exercise their free will—often rejecting God's will for their lives. God should not be blamed! By their rebellion, they have put themselves beyond His help!

"But Deon," I hear some say, "Isn't the earth the Lord's and the fullness thereof? Doesn't He own the cattle on a thousand hills, the wealth in every mine?" Absolutely right! The whole caboodle is His, and He has put His children in charge of it. *"The heavens belong to the LORD, but He has given the earth to all humanity."* (Psa 115:16).

The question is: As the creator of everything, can there be anything at all that He doesn't own? There is something. He doesn't own our free will. He doesn't even want us to give up our free will. He allows us to choose. We can shut Him out of our lives if we wish. We are at liberty to choose heaven or hell—a free choice He will never retract. He prizes the freedom He gave us, because without it, how could He be sure that our love for Him is genuine? The option for hate and indifference must always exist— without it, sincerity in love cannot be known. Love given under compulsion is not love at all. So, He had to risk rejection in order to know that our love for Him is true!

Sovereignty, free will, dominion and authority are first cousins. They come in one and the same package. Each aspect validating the other. He created a family, but rather than impose Himself upon them, He purposely granted them freedom to choose. Why? He desired a genuine relationship!

In empowering His children to take care of the earth, He gave them full control of a small part of His vast domain. If the chaotic condition of the Planet under our management is anything to go by, then we must admit, our management leaves much to be desired! But this is the risk He chose to take. How did mankind use their freedom? Sadly, much of mankind abused it to hate Him, going so far as to murder God's only Son.

But, if the Earth is man's domain, how is God going to get it back when Jesus returns? Simple—God will send His Son to earth to reign. Never forget, He is the One who became a "man". Isn't it interesting that it is Jesus, the human aspect of the triune God who will continue to reign as "man" over man's domain? Our earthly reign will never end—together with Him, we will reign for a thousand years. And that's not where it ends—the restored earth will last forever!

As much as God may want to intervene on Planet Earth, He stands by patiently waiting for us, the sovereign princes He put in charge of the Planet, to grant Him permission. As unquestionably omnipotent as He is, He still requires the permission of mere earthlings. With unflinching declarations of faith, they invite His intervention. Without our express permission, He has no legal right to intervene. This very moment, He is patiently waiting for your permission. Isn't it time to play your part? A good time to pray, *"Thy will be done on Earth as it is done in Heaven"*.

He said that it is His will that all should be saved, and that not one should be lost. Well, if as some might say, His will is always accomplished on earth, then why isn't everybody saved? It is significant that only those who choose salvation actually get salvation. He needs our collaboration and permission to save us, heal us, bless us, provide for us etc. It is not because He is a gentleman that He waits for our permission, although He certainly is, it is because He, in His sovereign plan, respects the sovereignty He granted mankind.

If I give you my house as a gift and you take legal transfer of it, I no longer have dominion over it. I am no longer permitted to use my front door key to enter your home. If I walked in without invitation, I would be trespassing and be in trouble with the law. But it's different if you invite me in.

I no longer have the right to dictate to you how you should landscape your garden. If I don't like the colour of the roses you planted, I have no right to uproot them and plant daisies. My sovereignty over the house ended the day you took transfer. Your sovereignty over that property allows you to make both good and bad decisions concerning your property, and I am powerless to interfere. Even if I knew that you were making a bad decision, like uprooting the beautiful garden I so lovingly landscaped, to cover it with drab cement, I have no right to prevent you doing so. You have a right to ruin your house if it suits you. The title deed over your property ensures your sovereignty over it. Wreck it if you will— you don't have to answer to anybody.

My sovereignty over that property ended. If I wanted to help you with landscaping, the most I could do would be to offer my services, but unless you accepted my offer, I would remain powerless to help you.

Sovereign God had a plan to save humanity, but He didn't have permission to interfere with the very sovereignty He had granted humanity. The dominion that was given to Adam, is now in the hands of Adam's many descendants.

Unholy men can break their word, but a holy God does not have that luxury. His integrity is His guarantee—He is holy! As much as He may wish to, He can no longer use His key to open our front door—not even to save us from self-destruction. Instead He stands outside patiently knocking. In the same way that I may offer my landscaping skills, but must wait for your invitation, He made His offer, and waits for our invitation. He must have our permission. Isn't it amazing that the Emperor of the vast universe allows mere mortals to override His sovereign will?

In order to solve man's dilemma, He had to become a man, but He couldn't even do that without man's permission. When the archangel visited Mary to tell her of God's plan to save mankind, His plan could not go ahead without Mary's express permission. Of course, He knew Mary's heart and so trusted her to grant Him authorisation. Mary replied to the arch angel, *"Be it unto me according to thy word"* (Luke 1:38 KJV). This was all the authority God needed for His son to become a man, and for mankind to be saved by a man—a perfect Man!

God seeks permission to intervene in all our flawed doings. He is more willing to give than we are to receive, but He honours the legality of our sovereign dominion. Of course, in doing so, He runs the risk of being left out in the cold, as is often the case.

You might be thinking, "It's different for God. He can do whatever He pleases." Really? Then why is He standing outside your door patiently knocking? *"Look! I stand at the door and knock. If you hear My voice and open the door, I will come in, and we will share a meal together as friends"* (Rev 3:20). Why doesn't He just open the door, step inside and take over? The answer is that He doesn't have a key. He left the key in our custody when He transferred dominion to us.

When I was a kid, my grandmother had a copy of a painting in her lounge. It didn't mean much to me then. Now I know it to be one of Christianity's most famous paintings. You may have seen it. Jesus is in a garden at night knocking on what appears to be a big oak door.

The painter, Holman Hunt, invited his friends and family to witness the unveiling of his masterpiece. Quietness descended over the group as each person stood, moved by the magnificence of the artwork, drinking in the deep feelings conveyed through the paining. Then one by one, they began to comment on what impressed them most about it. One friend said hesitantly, "Uh, Holman—it's a beautiful painting. But—well, didn't you forget something?"

"What did I forget?" The friend replied, "The handle. There's no handle on the door." To which the artist replied, "Oh no! I didn't forget the handle. When Jesus knocks on the door of your heart—the handle is on the INSIDE."

Not even Almighty God overrides the independence He gave us. He has such a high regard for our sovereignty that He would rather be shut out in the cold of night than force His way in uninvited. You may be saying that He can require our souls in a flash. Undoubtedly! But He can't even kill us without first revealing it to His prophets.

He does nothing on this earth without our invitation. *"Indeed, the Sovereign LORD never does anything until He reveals His plans to His servants the prophets"* (Amos 3:7). If He says that He never does anything without first revealing it to His prophets, then you can bet your life on it! He will never make an exception! He doesn't do it this way without good reason. He does it, because He must have a person with earthly dominion to give Him permission to intervene. By the way, in this sense, we are all prophets. Our words, our day-to-day speech, our confessions and declarations either prophesy words of faith or doubt—either way, they have spiritual consequences!

Mothers tell their children, "You will catch a cold if you walk barefoot on the cold cement." It is prophetic. They will catch a cold. Teachers tell difficult pupils, "You will never amount to anything." It's prophetic. They will never amount to anything. When God created, He used nothing more than words mixed with faith. When there was darkness, He didn't say "darkness", He said "light". Immediately darkness transformed into light. The Bible tells us to be imitators of God. After all, we are His children, and children imitate their parents. Just as He is the Creator, He made us to be creators, with a small "c" of course. Our day to day words carry prophetic power for both good and ill.

"For verily I say unto you, That whosoever shall say unto this mountain, Be thou removed, and be thou cast into the sea; and shall not doubt in his heart, but shall believe that those things which he saith shall come to pass; he shall have whatsoever he saith" (Mark 11:23 KJV). This scripture is not referring to prayer, it's referring to "saying". The last part is frightening. *"He shall have whatever he saith"*. Good words equal good creations, and bad words equal bad creations. Our present circumstances

are the sum-total of what we have spoken in the past. If you are in a mess and wondering how you got there, perhaps you will find the answer in the words you have spoken.

Certain medical conditions are more prevalent in certain geographical regions of the world. There seemed to be no logical explanation for this phenomenon. Then medical science made the connection. They found that regional ailments could be linked to regional idiomatic use of language. In the day to day common usage of any language, people in one region may say that someone is a pain in the neck. Neck problems would be more prevalent in that region. In another region people may more commonly say that someone is a pain in the butt. Haemorrhoids would be more prevalent in that region.

It goes much further than that. Families bring both good and bad upon themselves by the way they talk to each other. Even the words we speak to ourselves have both good and bad ramifications. When we are caught speeding, we may turn on ourselves in accusation, "You stupid idiot! You know the traffic cops always sit there." If we continue with this kind of self-recrimination, what chance is there of preserving our self-esteem? We end up collaborating with the *"accuser of the brethren"*, doing a number on our self-confidence! We destroy personal value with derogatory self-talk, making ourselves easy pickings for our enemy. He just stands back rubbing his hands in glee—his work is done—we have done it for him!

When God says that He always tells His plans to His prophets, it is for the purpose of getting men to declare God's will, thus inviting His intervention. The angels stand by waiting for our signal to intervene. Prophetic declarations grant them permission to go into action. Without our invitation, God simply has no right to override our sovereign free-will. He abides by His own laws—honouring the legality of the sovereignty He granted us. After all, it was His idea to give it to us in the first place—His idea not to interfere.

You may say that you have experienced God's sovereign intervention without having prayed for it. It may seem that way to you, but for it to be so, He would have had to break His promise. And we all know that He never breaks promises—not even to make an exception for His most beloved. If you didn't personally initiate a miraculous God-intervention, then who did? If God couldn't use someone who knows about your problem, He might have to wake a long-lost uncle in the middle of the night to pray in the Spirit, but He could not move on your behalf without first being invited by mankind to do so.

If we don't see it that way, we will most likely blame God by saying that the world's catastrophes are God's will. We hear religious people saying things like "God knows best" when an innocent person is shot dead, caught in the crossfire of bank robbers. Really! It doesn't take a rocket scientist to know that it wasn't God's will to rob a bank. Neither was it His will for anyone to die in the crossfire of criminal activity.

In the example of the toddler being run over by a drunken driver while riding her tricycle on the sidewalk—God didn't arrange the drinking spree, and He certainly didn't want him to drive his car in a state of inebriation. Religion says, "God is teaching us something through this." Please tell me what lesson the dead toddler learnt from this catastrophe. Sure we know that God is able to turn into good what Satan meant for our harm, but this does not for a moment mean that we should blame God with all manner of religious mumbo jumbo like, *The Lord gives and the Lord takes away, blessed be the name of the Lord.*" Although Job said this, he later repented for saying it. The book of Job is a record of the folly of ungodly wisdom.

Why can't God just go ahead and save everybody? With dominion comes free-will. God cannot go against our free-will. But the fact that He can't do certain things does not infer that He is no longer omnipotent. It infers that He is honourable, honouring the legality of the sovereign dominion He conferred upon us. God's idea for creating us in the first place was to put us in charge of the Earth, and to have the pleasure of fellowshipping with willing participants. Willingness is paramount! Obviously, the moment affection is coerced out of us, as religion requires, affection becomes fraudulent!

God wanted to reconcile men to himself, but He needed a body like any other man to gain a legal right to do so. A human body allowed Him to share man's sovereign authority—it gave Him the necessary credentials and legal right to recover man's dominion from Satan. Because man lost his dominion, only man could retrieve it; not God! Even when He walked the Planet, He needed man's permission to perform the miraculous on them. When He healed the sick, He did not do it as God; He did it as a man.

Jesus established His identity as a man by regularly referring to Himself as the Son of Man, rarely conceding that He is also the Son of God. Even as a man, with man's authority, there were times when He was unable to perform miracles. "Come on now—you can't be serious! This is almighty God, the One who created the whole universe. Are you seriously telling us that He was 'unable' to do any good thing? Are you implying that the will of imperfect man can override the will of a perfect God?" Yes, indeed! It happened in Nazareth. The question is: "Who was it that prevented the omnipotent God of the universe from doing any good in Nazareth?" The answer is "men"—men in their unbelief! Men's sovereign will overrode God's sovereign will on Earth. When He couldn't obtain men's cooperation through their faith, as in the case of Nazareth; mere puny men had effectively hamstrung the Almighty God from performing miracles in mankind's territory. Clearly, mere mortals had prevented the Almighty from doing His will.

Before we jump to conclusions and judge these men for their lack of faith, we should ponder and recall the many times we have tied His hands in like manner. We do this by choosing doubt and unbelief rather than immovable faith. When our bodies tell us that we are sick, the Word tells us that by His stripes we were healed. When we give more weight to what the pain in our bodies tell us, than to what the Word of God tells us, we debilitate our faith, thus preventing almighty God from healing us. When this happens, we should not be surprised—it's how the people of Nazareth shut Jesus' work down. Judging by the general lack of miracles in many modern-day churches, I think it is safe to say that we are no different to the Nazarenes. Aren't we supposed to be doing greater miracles than Jesus as a matter of routine? Didn't Jesus say we would?

Satan does all he can to usurp man's sovereign authority. Without it he is no more than a defeated wimp. Do we really understand that His defeat at Calvary was absolute and complete? Now the only way he can obtain any power is when we foolishly hand it to him. When we see his handiwork in the chaos, loss, lack, sickness, oppression, damaged relationships etc, let us not forget that he wouldn't have any authority at all if we hadn't given it to him with ill-chosen words of fear, doubt and unbelief! Job went through a lot of pain—he lost everything he had, including his family. How did Satan obtain the power to cause so much chaos? Job explained it. He said that the very thing that he had feared had come upon him. Fear was all the permission Satan needed. But while we are standing in emphatic, unshakable faith, he simply cannot take a single thing from us. Let us not give him an inch of leeway; not a single fear to work with.

James says that a man whose faith wavers will receive nothing. As much as it is God's will to do us good, He cannot do what he wants without us declaring our faith with unshakable confidence. This very moment, He is awaiting our legal permission.

An oft quoted verse is: *"For I know the plans I have for you," says the Lord. "They are plans for good and not for disaster, to give you a future and a hope"* (Jer 29:11 NLT).

This is God's will for you, but even though He promised it to you, He cannot perform His most sacred will in your life without your permission. You have the power to thwart God's good intentions for you. The very next verse illustrates that you have the power to allow or prevent Him from doing His Will. *"In those days when you pray, I will listen."* Prayer is our way of inviting God into our disasters. Without prayer, even though He is Almighty God, He cannot intervene. God won't use His omnipotence to override our will—He honours every word He said and places a high value on the freedom He gave us!

In the 1980's our church experienced an awakening on a scale that took us all by surprise. We had been cruising along for many years with an average church attendance of about fifty. Our new facility could comfortably seat three hundred and fifty, and at a push, seven hundred. We had plenty of room to grow, but it just wasn't happening. Then something quite miraculous occurred. Without any special prayer meetings for revival on our part, suddenly we were unable to accommodate the crowds. Half an hour before scheduled starting time, the ushers were turning people away at the church door, suggesting that they try coming a little earlier next time.

You know that a revival is real when most of the congregation is comprised of previously unchurched youth whose parents are not believers. The fervency of their newly found faith took the older members by surprise. With their insatiable hunger for the Word of God, the miraculous soon became the norm!

We couldn't put the revival down to better services, better preaching, better anything. We couldn't even take credit for having special prayer for revival. We were profoundly undeserving of a supernatural visitation. For all intents and purposes, this appeared to be entirely gratuitous—a sovereign move of God. We had no other explanation for it. Overwhelmed and grateful, we rejoiced in God's grace. To this day, people still speak of it as a sovereign move of God.

That it was a move of God is not in question. The only question is, was it really a sovereign move? If God said that He does nothing unless He first reveals it to His prophets, then nothing on the Earth takes place by His sovereign will alone. His intervention is always in response to what we do with what He reveals to us. Who are His prophets? None other than everyday ordinary believers. He moves when we declare His will. In other words, God moves on this earth in accordance with what we chose to declare of His sovereign will. Seeing that He never moves independently of us, how do we explain this revival? Surely it makes nonsense of this view!

What many in this church were not aware of was that the Student Christian Association of a local high school had invited an out-of-town evangelist to hold a series of meetings at their school. My sister, Joy, was president of that Association at the time. As a run-up to the campaign, they held 24 hour-a-day prayer meetings at my parents' home, praying for revival. This is where God's intervention was sought, and it was enough for Him to unleash a remarkable revival. God is just waiting for such a call from sovereign men and women. He is more ready to give than we are to receive, but His willingness can be thwarted by prayerlessness.

We have all heard people say, "If God blesses me, that will be great, but I am content if He doesn't." These folk don't realise that they will not see God's intervention, because they have decided not to declare His intervention with unwavering words of faith. Even some church leaders take this casual approach to revival. "If revival comes, great! But if it doesn't, that's also okay", they say. As much as God would love to intervene, He can't—He waits for their invitation.

Unless we know what took place behind the scenes—the kind of prayer, confession and prophecy preceding a particular move of God, we are likely to assume that God's moves are purely sovereign. It may lead us to conclude that He just randomly chooses to do whatever He wants to, whenever He wants to. But according to His way of doing things, somebody must have prayed, declared, confessed or prophesied! We might not even know who prayed into our circumstances. We just experienced the hand of God miraculously moving circumstances to our benefit. Although we might not have prayed into the situation, behind the scenes, there may have been a praying mother, or a complete stranger who accidentally bumped into us in the street, or perhaps someone on the other side of the Planet, woken in the middle of the night to pray in the spirit—someone not even aware of our predicament. God has His prayer warriors in the most unlikely of places. But why wait to find out whether someone else has been obedient to pray for us? Let's get on with it and pray—declaring God's will—it's written in red in our Bibles.

You might be saying, "Now you have taken this too far, Deon. You are putting God in a box." Well, I've got to admit that I don't know everything there is to know about God, but I know enough about Him to know for sure that if He says anything, we can bank it. If He could break even one of His promises, then none of His promises are trustworthy. We simply wouldn't know which promises He would break next. But those of us who are entirely convinced of His integrity, we know with absolute certainty that we can put our lives on the line for every word He has ever uttered. If He said that He does nothing without first telling His prophets, then we can rest assured that He will never do a single thing without first telling us. There can never be an exception to this rule. It isn't my box. I didn't write Amos 3:7.

What about the day of Pentecost? Was this most pivotal of all spiritual awakenings not a sovereign move of God? After all, it happened exactly as

Jesus predicted. Well that's exactly it! He prophesied it and people prayed—something they were doing a lot of at the time. In fact, they were gathered for prayer on the very day that the outpouring broke out.

Jesus wasn't the only prophet to predict this event; it had been foreseen long before by Old Testament prophets, and they prophesied it into existence. Even Pentecost had to be prophesied and prayed for before it could become a reality.

Although Abram received a promise that he would be a father of many nations, he remained childless for many years—way past his wife's childbearing age. Imagine an old dried out wrinkled prune, and you get the idea of how sensual Sarai must have been in her old age. With all her sensuality long passed, she stood little chance of arousing Abram's sexuality. No wonder she laughed at the angel of the Lord's promise that she would bear a child. Their passionate past was well and truly beyond its 'use by' date.

Although Abram seriously needed a miracle, even sovereign God Almighty, with all the power in the universe, could not give him a family without his permission. How did God get Abram to play along? In the mind of any reasonable person, it simply could not happen. And not even God almighty could step in unless He had Abram's express permission. How could He possibly get around such insurmountable odds? To Abram, the very thought of producing a son was ludicrous! Despite this, God had to find a way to get Him to speak the miracle into existence.

Here's how He caused Abram to change the way he was thinking; He did it by changing the pattern of his speech. A change of name would be enough to do it. He changed Abram's name to Abraham, meaning father of many nations. Every time he introduced himself, he would have to say, "How do you do, I'm father of many nations". In doing so, he would be declaring the promise into existence—granting God authority to intervene supernaturally. Did you know that God could be that sneaky? The rest is history! He fathered one whole nation through his son Isaac, followed by the adoption of every New Covenant believer on the face of the Planet. This would be wrought through his descendent, Jesus!

Believers often find it difficult to say that something is opposite to what they see. They feel that it's as good as lying. Imagine Abraham introducing himself, "I am Father of many nations".

"Oh yes! How many children do you have?"

"Well none, actually". If Abraham was not prepared to endure this kind of embarrassment, he would not have obtained the promise, a promise that played the most pivotal role in pre-New Covenant history.

Gideon was told by the angel that he was a *"mighty man of valour"* while it was obvious that he was anything but a mighty man of valour—hiding as he was, scared to death of the enemy. The Angel wasn't lying; he was prophesying, giving Gideon a new image of himself to live up to. He could not win the battle with his poor self-image—he needed to see himself in a new light. He was chosen to challenge an overwhelmingly bigger army than his own. It was a battle that would go down in history as the most uneven contest of all time!

Jesus changed Simon's name to Peter, meaning rock, when he was anything but a rock, having just denied that he even knew Jesus. This was at a time when Jesus needed his loyalty more than ever. Here was a yellow bellied, lily livered, unreliable wimp, being renamed by Jesus as "dependable as a rock". Peter needed to declare his own unshakable stability in order to awaken stability within himself. Jesus required Peter to have this kind of dependability before He could entrust him with the responsibility of leading His entire church.

Scripture is loaded with examples of prophecy preceding decisive moves of God. There was Noah, Joseph, Moses, Joshua, Daniel and so many more.

If we are Sovereign, Can We Change God's Will?

I have often heard it said that prayer does not change God; it changes us. There is a half-truth to this statement. We certainly do change for the better when we spend time in His presence. We have all experienced upliftment, encouragement, empowerment and revitalised strength to meet challenges after spending time on our knees. But are mere mortals really able to change the will of the mighty God of the entire universe? To the religious mind, even such a suggestion would be regarded as heresy. How dare puny men even entertain such a thought! Well then, what does the Bible have to say about this?

When God told Abraham that He was about to destroy Sodom, Abraham pleaded with Him to spare the city if there were a certain number of righteous people living there. God agreed. God's will had been changed by a mere mortal's request. Unfortunately, Abraham didn't get the numbers right, but the fact remains that God was willing to change His mind.

After Isaiah, the prophet, had given God's message to King Hezekiah that he would die from his sickness, the king turned on his bed towards the wall and prayed. His prayer caused the prophet Isaiah to stop in his tracks, turn around and return to tell Hezekiah that God had granted him an extra fifteen years. Again, God's will had been changed by the prayer of a mere mortal. He is prepared to listen to our reasoning, and ready to change His will in so far as it concerns our domain.

Bear in mind that this was the Old Testament. In the New Testament, God takes this to a whole different level; He asks what our desire is. He says, *"What things so ever ye desire."* We don't have to change His mind about anything, He has already decided to go along with our desires.

Of course, there are other types of prayer where God's will is not known and must be sought. In those cases, we are at liberty to seek God's desire and plan. But that isn't the type of prayer He referred to in Mark 11:24. Here it is not His desire, but ours for which we are to pray. In this scripture His desire is to fulfil our desires, not merely our needs.

In the New Testament we don't have to change His mind about sickness; He has already made up His mind on that issue. In our day and age, neither Jesus nor the Father heals sicknesses and diseases anymore—that's because Jesus has already finished healing all sicknesses. The stripes He took on His back were enough to heal every sickness for all time. As a result, sickness cannot withstand a believer's declaration of healing, when declared in faith in Jesus' name.

If we don't accept that we were healed by His stripes (past tense), we will pray incorrectly and fruitlessly. Expecting Him to heal us is a prayer that He just cannot answer. Just as God doesn't have to go back to the cross to save additional people, He doesn't have to go back to the whip master to be whipped afresh for additional healing. Either we accept that we *"were"* healed, and therefore are healed, or we must put up with sickness.

In the great commission, Jesus commanded His disciples to heal the sick themselves. Peter's prayer for the sick is a classic example for each and every one of us to emulate. When the lame man at the Gate Beautiful begged for money as they were passing, Peter replied: *"Silver and gold have I none; but such as I have give I thee: In the name of Jesus Christ of Nazareth rise up and walk"* (Act 3:6 KJV). He didn't ask God to do something, he told the lame man to do something. God didn't have to do a thing! In saying, "I'll give you what I have", Peter wasn't giving the lame man something God had; he was giving him something he himself had!

The healing that Peter had within himself, is no different to the healing deposited within every born-again believer. The same power that raised Jesus from the dead, dwells within each of us. We are endowed with all the healing we could ever desire. No need to obtain it from God. It is a fait accompli, ready and available to be appropriated by faith. There is only one way to appropriate it, and that is through words declared in faith. Unless we see it as a done deal, we are likely to pray amiss.

God looks for people who will stand in the gap for others—people who will plead with Him to change His will. *"And I sought for a man among them, that should make up the hedge, and stand in the gap before me for the land, that I should not destroy it: but I found none"* (Eze 22:30 KJV). God was about to destroy the land. It was His sovereign will to do so, but He looked for a man who would convince Him otherwise. Whatever that man would decide to ask, God would do. In this scripture we see that God was hoping to find someone who (dare I say it?) would twist His arm (metaphorically speaking) and cause Him to change His mind and spare the land that He was about to destroy.

God allowed mere mortals to influence Him. From this it is clear that He places much weight on man's sovereign dominion over the Earth.

Under the New Covenant, it is clear that He has made up His mind to endow us with an abundance of benefits. We don't need to beg Him for salvation, healing, physical provisions, joy, peace etc. He has already decided. Now it is merely a matter of us declaring, "Yea and amen!"

What about Luke 11:7,8: *"And suppose he calls out from his bedroom, 'Don't bother me. The door is locked for the night, and my family and I are all in bed. I can't help you.' But I tell you this—though he won't do it for friendship's sake, if you keep knocking long enough, he will get up and give you whatever you need because of your shameless persistence."*

Traditional thought on this scripture is that we should continue asking God until He gives in. That's not what this scripture is telling us to do. Jesus wasn't drawing a parallel between this man and God, He was drawing a contrast between them. If we see this as a parallel, we will not be able to obey Jesus' instruction to receive the answer to our prayer at the very same instant that we pray. *"I tell you, you can pray for anything, and if you believe that you've received it, it will be yours"* (Mark 11:24). If Luke 11:7,8 was meant to be a parallel, it would contradict Mark 11:24. But contradictions are not possible in the word of God.

Religion has misled us on this issue to the point of cancelling our prayers. We cancel our first prayer by praying a second time for the same thing. In other words, our second prayer becomes an admission that we did not obey Jesus' command to receive at the precise moment of our first prayer. Our third prayer then cancels our second prayer, and so the cycle of cancelled prayer continues. Sure, we should continue to pray, but subsequent prayer ought to take on the form of thanksgiving for what we received upon uttering our first prayer.

But there is another issue: Are we really meant to identify with the beggar in this story? If we are the beggar, we would be forced to conclude that God is unwilling to bless us. We would have to wear Him down with incessant nagging and persistent pestering until He reluctantly relents, gives in and gives us a handout to get us off His back. This is certainly not consistent with the God of the Bible—He is more willing to give than we are to receive.

Where do we fit into this parable? Are we the beggar out in the cold, or the child tucked safely in bed? Surely, we are the child! After all, we are children of God, aren't we? You can be quite sure that we didn't go to bed on an empty stomach, and we certainly didn't have to beg for our supper.

When we read the Old Testament, it is important to remember that, although God never changes, He relates to New Covenant believers in a different way. We no longer stone offenders, nor offer animal sacrifices, and by the same token, we no longer have to ask for stuff that He has already conferred upon us in terms of a rock-solid covenant. We simply draw from what He has deposited within us. We are wall to wall Holy Spirit!

The Kingdom

"Fear not, little flock; for it is your Father's good pleasure to give you the kingdom" (Luke 12:32KJV).

The good news is that God doesn't give us Kingdom privileges grudgingly. The New Living Translation says, *"it gives your Father great happiness."* Don't you just love making God happy? Then come fetch your privileges—don't delay—come make His day!"

"Yes Lord, but I don't want to bother You with my piffling hassles."

"Bother Me? You're kidding Me! Do you really want to rob me of My pleasures? I'm trying to get good things to you; please don't spoil my fun."

"But You wouldn't be interested in something as unimportant as helping me to find a parking."

"Who told you that? Spoiling My kids gives meaning to farther-hood—what a joy to see My most treasured darlings enjoying My special treats!

"Thank you Lord for blessing me."

He replies, "No, the pleasure is all mine! Thank you for allowing me the honour of spoiling my beloved ones. Please give me another opportunity real soon—I can hardly wait to lavish more affection upon you."

The Kingdom of God is not in a particular place, it's wherever the subjects of His Kingdom live under His Lordship.

"Seek the Kingdom of God above all else, and live righteously, and He will give you everything you need." (Mat 6:33)

You don't qualify for the second part of this verse until you have qualified for the first. He only promises to give you everything you need after you have sought His rule over your every decision. Under the King's rulership, the responsibility of providing for you shifts from you to the King! Yours is the easy part—it is to give up your right to do things your way. You don't have to worry about the difficult part—the provision of all your needs—the King will take care of that! While He is in charge, He takes full responsibility for His subjects.

The Kingdom of God has no lack. Lack belongs to another kingdom. Outside the Kingdom, it is a matter of dog eat dog—every man for himself. Within the Kingdom we are under God's lordship, a place where everything runs in perfect sync. We don't participate in the ups and downs of the world's economy; we participate in the stable economy of the kingdom, where our personal wellbeing is provided for according to His abundant riches in glory.

This being so, why are Christians often in lack? Would you believe that most Christians live outside of the parameters of the Kingdom?

"Are you saying that they are not going to heaven, Deon?" No. In the sweet by and by, they will discover that they had been in the Kingdom all along yet failed to participate in the enormous privileges available to them. Let us ask ourselves: Do we have irrefutable evidence of living by Kingdom privileges? Bear in mind, we are not saved for the purpose of going to heaven, although we are certainly going there; we are saved for the purpose of establishing God's Kingdom here on Earth. He has assigned us to reign over circumstances by His authority.

We each have our own earthly colonies of the kingdom to rule over while here on Earth. God ordained it to be so when He gave the Planet to Adam and his descendants to reign over. Now we have a choice, either to rule alone, or in alliance with the *"King of all kings and Lord of all lords"* (1 Tim 6:15). Who are the lords referred to in this scripture? It is us! We are lords, and He is only Lord of us when we, the lords of our earthly domains, make him the supreme Lord over ourselves and our dominions. In doing so, our personal kingdoms become part of the commonwealth of the Kingdom of God. Let's not kid ourselves, we do not participate in Kingdom privileges unless we live by the Kingdom's rules.

Here's the choice: Either to live by the world's rules—fighting for our rights, asserting ourselves to get anywhere, or to live by the Kingdom's rules where the King provides for all our needs.

What are the rules of the kingdom? It's all summed up in one rule: It is to adopt "GOD'S WAY OF DOING THINGS".

World's Way	*God's Way*
Take whatever you can to get whatever you want	Give whatever you can to get whatever you want
Exalt yourself to get anywhere	Humble yourself to get anywhere
Judge others in order to look good	Forgive others—you are already good
Exalt yourself	Esteem others higher than yourself
Hate the unlovable	Love the unlovable
Seek revenge upon those who have hurt you	Seek the blessing of God upon those who have hurt you

Retaliate	Turn the other cheek
Say you are sick	Say you are healed
Say you are in lack	Say, *"My God shall supply all my need according to His riches in glory"*
Say you can't do it	Say *"I can do all things through Christ"*
Say you are defeated	Say, *"I am always led in triumphant procession by Christ Jesus"*
Say, "Under the circumstances, I'm okay"	Say, "Circumstances are under my feet, because everything is under Jesus' feet and I am part of the body of Christ"

There are far too many differences to list here.

If this is not our personal experience, then our Kingdom privileges are going to go by unused. Sadly, this is the case with far too many believers. Although all are in the Kingdom, some live as though they are not—satisfied with a ticket to heaven, yet content to live below their blood bought privileges. But half-baked faith is not going to move mountains—not even a half-baked mountain! Faith is not optional; it is the one and only legal currency of the kingdom. As with any purchase, nothing can be bought without currency. Make good use of your currency—His favour awaits—withdraw whatever you wish.

God's way of doing things sounds like the exact opposite to the world's way, doesn't it? The book of Proverbs is jam packed with opposites—a whole book of Kingdom principles running contrary to logic. When logic sees a problem; faith sees a solution!

So many of God's wonderful people get caught up in the flurry of striving for the Kingdom through diligent service to the church. More meetings, more duties and more responsibilities. As good as these are, kingdom privileges cannot be earned. They have already been earned for us! It is not what we do that gets His attention; it is how immovable our faith is! A matter of adopting HIS WAY OF DOING THINGS. If His blessings can't be earned with good works, then what will motivate us to do good works? Here's the good news—when we discover the depth of His love, mercy, grace and good works follow without persuasion!

"A good person produces good things from the treasury of a good heart, and an evil person produces evil things from the treasury of an evil heart" (Mat 12:35). Did you get that? Once our hearts have been changed by His grace, it is not a matter of making an effort to do good works; it is a matter of discovering that we are doing good works, and we can give no explanation for it!

This is how Paul described the world's way: *"When you follow the desires of your sinful nature, the results are very clear: sexual immorality, impurity, lustful pleasures, idolatry, sorcery, hostility, quarreling, jealousy, outbursts of anger, selfish ambition, dissension, division, envy, drunkenness, wild parties, and other sins like these. Let me tell you again, as I have before, that anyone living that sort of life will not inherit the Kingdom of God"* (Gal 5:19-21).

This is how he described the Kingdom's way: *"But the Holy Spirit produces this kind of fruit in our lives: love, joy, peace, patience, kindness, goodness, faithfulness, gentleness, and self-control. There is no law against these things!"* (Gal 5:22, 23).

Although spiritually, we transitioned from the kingdom of this world into the kingdom of God in a flash, mental transition takes longer. The process is never complete. It involves paradigm shifts way down in the depth of our hearts. Those who attempt the transition through modifying their behaviour, never get too far. It takes love of the extreme kind to get through to hearts.

A heart surrendered to the Holy Spirit is a Spirit led heart. Once this is done, no further behavioural modification is required—changed hearts just don't behave the same.

The danger is that we may try to do what the Spirit has promised to do for us, and then wonder why we keep slipping back into our same old embarrassing ways. But works of the flesh are certainly not fruit of the Spirit. If we have achieved "holiness" through personal striving, we have achieved nothing at all. This is not fruit of the Spirit; it is just self-managed-righteousness—nothing better than "filthy rags" in God's sight.

We're not supposed to act like Christians—we are already Christians. Acting, is not being genuine; it is fraudulent! We may be able to bluff each other, but we cannot bluff ourselves, and we certainly cannot bluff God.

Salvation comes with kingdom privileges, but we don't walk in our privileges unless we take the trouble to activate them. They are activated by doing things God's way. While we reserve the right to call the shots, He is not in control. Kingdoms are ruled by kings. We can only claim to be true Kingdom citizens when we are allowing God to be Lord over our every decision. When this happens, His way of doing things becomes our way of doing things.

Do you want direction for your life? Nobody is without direction in His Kingdom. Do you want God's plan for your life? Everything runs to plan in His Kingdom. Do you want God's will to be done in your life? Allow His will to be accomplished. Do you want God's provisions? There is no lack in His Kingdom.

We don't have to go to heaven to have His will done, we simply do everything the way He does them. *"Let Your will be done on earth as it is in heaven."* When we pray these words, we are asking for the same order that exists in heaven, to exist in our lives here on earth. Just as He rules in heaven, we rule on the Planet under His supreme Lordship. If there is no sickness and lack in heaven, then there is no reason for sickness and lack to exist where we live.

"Once I was young, and now I am old. Yet I have never seen the godly abandoned or their children begging for bread" (Psalm 37:25). The godly are certainly not sinless. As much as they would wish not to sin, they cannot deny that they do. Yet they remain in right standing with God. They have no need to beg God for anything. They simply receive, without pleading, whatever the King has provided for His subjects. Each are in charge of their allocated colonies of the heavenly Kingdom on the Planet. Their divine dominion exists by permission under the absolute lordship of God. By delegated authority, they rule over sickness and lack in precisely the same way that Jesus did!

Rulership is not for sissies; it's for conquerors! Not ordinary conquerors; *"more than conquerors"!* This is who we are through Christ. If we are not fighting, we are not reigning in our colony of the Kingdom, and Satan will look for gaps in our defences. Give him half a chance and he will mess with our plans—he is determined to steal, kill and destroy! We do not fight to get victory; we fight to enforce the victory that has already been won for us by Jesus.

Religion is man's search for the Kingdom. Why on earth would we be searching for the Kingdom? He has already given it to us! Our responsibility is to seek out GOD'S WAY OF DOING THINGS within His Kingdom. He didn't send a Messiah to bring mankind into the bondage of religion; He sent Him to release us from religion's deathly grip. He made the great exchange—freedom in place of bondage—decisive kingdom reigning in place of domination!

Jesus had no intention of starting a new religion, in fact the very reason He came was to put an end to all religion once and for all. He replaced the structured protocol of religion with the spontaneity of true love—a divine romance—we love Him in response to His love for us!

This being the case, how do we explain why divine romance reverted back to burdensome religion? Men, who failed to move in the supernatural power of God, invented a set of rituals to mimic the real deal. Unfortunately, anything that isn't real is counterfeit, and true love does not fare well on phoniness. According to Jesus, worship must be done in spirit and in truth.

Sadly, with time, the pleasure of a passionate love affair with the King was reduced to a cold set of religious rules and Sunday ceremonial rituals. You may say that you do not belong to a ritualistic church. But that is debatable. A ritual is defined as an established or prescribed pattern of observance. Isn't that a good description of most modern-day church programmes?

Is God Teaching us a Lesson?

When Jesus encountered hurting humanity, He never once put their illnesses, blindness, handicaps or demon possessions down to the will of God. He never even suggested that God had allowed them to experience these afflictions in order to knock their characters into shape. But He regularly suggested that they were afflictions of Satan. He certainly never asked people what they did to deserve their predicament. Not even once did He give some religious reason that would ultimately benefit the afflicted person—never making a single suggestion that their predicament was part of God's overall plan for humanity's good. He just got on with it and healed them regardless. He healed all who were oppressed of the devil. Clearly, sickness is plain and simply the work of the devil, and Jesus came specifically to destroy the works of the devil (Acts 10:38).

The intents of three different agendas are being carried out upon the Earth. Seeing that God's will isn't always being carried out, we must accept that someone else's will is coming into play. If neither God's nor ours, then it is Satan's. Tragedies and afflictions are not consistent with Jesus' character, and because Jesus' character is identical to the Father's, we must conclude that tragedies and afflictions are not consistent with the Father's character. We should not be laying blame on God with pious Christianese platitudes. Rather, let's lay blame where blame is due. Don't let Satan get away with anything. Resist him and he will flee! Take a decisive stand against the havoc he has planned for you!

Seedtime and Harvest

In order to reign in life, we need to understand God's way of doing things, and to understand His way of doing things is to understand seedtime and harvest—it is the Kingdom way.

"While the earth remaineth, seedtime and harvest, and cold and heat, and summer and winter, and day and night shall not cease." (Gen 8:22 KJV)

This is the covenant God made with Noah. How do we know whether it still applies? If planet Earth is still spinning in the cosmos, the covenant of seedtime and harvest remains applicable—it cannot end during the Planet's existence. There is a common thread running through subsequent covenants, each confirming that this is still God's plan for the Planet. Jesus devoted much of His teaching to the subject of seedtime and harvest, and the apostles continued to put a strong emphasis on it. Few other subjects received as much attention in New Testament writings.

The great counterfeiter, Satan, has his own version of this truth to offer saints. It is so convincing that sincere Christians often mistake it for the genuine article. Just as no counterfeiter would produce a $3 bill, because that would be a dead giveaway, so he produces a counterfeit covenant so cleverly disguised that it cannot be distinguished from the genuine article. Sadly, his version of the covenant is even more acceptable to many believers than God's version. To be honest, his version is seemingly more pious than God's. Satan's version says that when you sow, you should do it from a pure heart that expects nothing in return. This noble sounding self-denying kindness has immense appeal to religious thinkers—it just sounds so magnanimous and virtuous. It's not as though Satan is offering something as obvious as sin. No, this noble standpoint sounds so much like a virtuous God—how can it possibly be wrong? Sadly, this is how easily unsuspecting believers are robbed of their covenant rights.

Wealth Promised

"But thou shalt remember the LORD thy God: for it is he that giveth thee power to get wealth, that he may establish his covenant which he swore unto thy fathers, as it is this day." (Deut 8:18 KJV).

A Covenant is a legal agreement setting out contractual obligations. It relies heavily upon the integrity of each contractual party to carry out its promises. God's integrity (His holiness) does not afford Him the luxury of reneging on promises. There are no escape clauses for Him—He bound Himself to create wealth for us. Seeing the terms of the promises are indelibly embedded in an unambiguous covenant, we can take Him at His word. He is not a man that He should lie—always true to His word—an integrity beyond reproach! Once He has made a promise, His holiness obliges Him to carry it out to the T. He is so serious about making us wealthy, that in Deuteronomy 8:18, He *"swore"* to do it!

That being the case, how do we explain the poverty of so many believers? The promised wealth only goes to those who dare to receive it by faith. Most Christians will forego God's generous gift, either through ignorance, or because this concept does not sit well with religious paradigms. Unfortunately for them, they miss a vital element of their relationship with their Father. Seeing that God only relates to mankind through covenants, to opt out of participating in His covenant of kindness, would be an atrocious act of ingratitude. How ungracious of us to slam the door in the face of the One bearing gifts! God is left standing outside, while we piously adopt a more religiously acceptable way than His.

Sadly, there are many religious frameworks that succeed only in robbing perfectly sincere children of God of their promised covenant rights, leaving them weak and ineffective in the realm of the miraculous. There is nothing godly about religion. I can only imagine that God hates religion with a passion—it keeps men at arm's length from His desire to enjoy their intimacy.

Religion is Satan's best attempt at counterfeiting divine relationships. Religion is his strongest ally—he promotes it, doing anything to distract us from relating to our Father by covenant! He knows that, without our covenant rights, we present no threat to his wicked work of killing, stealing and destroying. When we choose religion over grace, it is game over—another one bites the dust—the *"accuser of the brethren"* just rubs his hands in glee!

Just in case we are of the opinion that this promise ended with the introduction of the New Covenant, we are reassured that we have a better covenant with better promises. *"But now Jesus, our High Priest, has been given a ministry that is far superior to the old priesthood, for He is the One who mediates for us a far better covenant with God, based on better promises"* (Heb 8:6).

And if this is not enough to convince us, scripture shows us the lengths that Jesus went to in order to secure our wealth. *"You know the generous grace of our Lord Jesus Christ. Though He was rich, yet for your sakes*

He became poor, so that by His poverty He could make you rich" (2 Cor 8:9).

God so much wants us to become rich that He became poor to make it a reality. If you are thinking that the poverty of Jesus referred to here is spiritual poverty, not material poverty, think again. Jesus has never been spiritually poor, but He certainly lived materially poor compared to the wealth He came from. He left the awe-inspiring wealth of heaven, where gold is in such abundance that even the streets are paved with it. Very different to the dusty roads He trod in the Middle East.

"The blessing of the LORD makes a person rich, and He adds no sorrow with it" (Prov 10:22). Accompanying God's blessing is riches. In this sense, riches aren't only material wealth; every aspect of our lives is potentially enriched. In Proverbs 3:15,16, material wealth is more clearly defined, because it is distinguished by making separate mention of *"life"*, *"riches"* and *"honour"*. *"Wisdom is more precious than rubies; nothing you desire can compare with her. She offers you long life in her right hand, and riches and honor in her left"*. Three separate blessings, one of which is material wealth.

What was Jesus' purpose on earth? *"The thief's purpose is to steal and kill and destroy. My purpose is to give them a rich and satisfying life"* (John 10:10). These words were spoken by Jesus Himself. His purpose is to give us life bursting with abundance!

God has a favourite verse of scripture (I say this with a measure of tongue in cheek, but there is a strong emphasis here). He has one verse that He wishes we would benefit from more than any other verse—He wishes it *"above all things"*. *"Beloved, I wish above all things that thou mayest prosper and be in health, even as thy soul prospereth"* (3 John 1:2 KJV).

In this verse, the way that we prosper materially is to first prosper in our souls. God's material prosperity will not exceed our soul's prosperity.

Our souls are the thinking part of our triune beings. In other words, we are to first get our thinking in line with the Kingdom's way of doing things. *"But seek ye first the kingdom of God, and his righteousness; and all these things shall be added unto you"* (Mat 6:33).

If we are already in the Kingdom, what else is it about the Kingdom that He requires us to seek after? *"For the kingdom of God is … righteousness, and peace, and joy in the Holy Ghost"* (Rom 14:17). If we see this as a command, we will not recognise it as a promise, and before we know it, we will be side-tracked into performing for something that can only be obtained by faith. The acquisition of righteousness, peace and joy come without effort—they are the by-products of discovering the Kingdom's way of doing things.

In that case, what is the Kingdom's way of doing things? "Wisdom is more precious than rubies; nothing you desire can compare with her…" (Prov 3:15, 16). It is all about wisdom, and the Kingdom's wisdom is precisely opposite to worldly wisdom.

You may recognise a similarity between the following list and the list in the chapter on the Kingdom. We need to understand that the Kingdom's wisdom bears no resemblance to the world's wisdom—the world's way is the Kingdom's way in reverse!

World's Wisdom	*Kingdom's Wisdom*
Take in order to receive	Give in order to receive.
Retain what you've got when you're in lack.	Give away what you've got when you're in lack.

Degrade others in order to get ahead.	Promote others in order to get ahead.
Begrudge in order to take revenge.	Forgive in order to make room for God's vengeance.
Find love by demanding it.	Find love through giving it away.
Control others.	Release others.
Speak the problem.	Speak the solution.
Receive sickness.	Receive healing.
Allow circumstances to dictate our happiness.	Allow the joy of the Lord to dictate our happiness.
Hate the unlovable.	Love the unlovable.
Look out for our own best interests	Look out for the best interests of others.
Doing things our way.	Doing things God's way.

What is the Kingdom? This is how Jesus explained it: *"…The Kingdom of God is like a farmer who scatters seed on the ground. Night and day, while he's asleep or awake, the seed sprouts and grows, but he does not understand how it happens. The earth produces the crops on its own. First a leaf blade pushes through, then the heads of wheat are formed, and finally the grain ripens. And as soon as the grain is ready, the farmer comes and harvests it with a sickle, for the harvest time has come … How can I describe the Kingdom of God? What story should I use to illustrate it? It is like a mustard seed planted in the ground. It is the smallest of all seeds, but it becomes the largest of all garden plants; it grows long branches, and birds can make nests in its shade"* (Mark 4:26-32).

We cannot dismiss seedtime and harvest or call it optional when Jesus describes the very Kingdom of God as seedtime and harvest. Seedtime and harvest was the subject of much of His ministry—too many of His parables deal with this very theme, for us to ignore it.

Did you notice that Jesus said that the earth produces crops on its own? The earth has no option, it has to produce a harvest—God has decreed it! But even the earth cannot produce anything without seed.

Seeing that God is the King of His Kingdom, perhaps we should sow seed as He does. After all, the Bible requires us to be imitators of God. In that case, what are some of the principles He lives by?

Principle no I – Give in order to Receive (seed faith)

God set the example. *"For God so loved the world, that he gave his only begotten Son, that whosoever believeth in him should not perish, but have everlasting life"* (John 3:16). Contrary to the religious idea that we should not expect a return for our giving, God expected a huge return for His giving. He sowed one Son in order to reap gazillions of sons.

"I tell you the truth, unless a kernel of wheat is planted in the soil and dies, it remains alone. But its death will produce many new kernels—a plentiful harvest of new lives" (John 12:24). Here Jesus explains how God operates by seedtime and harvest. When He sowed His seed, Jesus, His seed had to die in the ground before it took on the power to change you and me and to bring Him a mother lode harvest of sons.

"Give, and you will receive. Your gift will return to you in full—pressed down, shaken together to make room for more, running over, and poured into your lap. The amount you give will determine the amount you get back" (Luke 6:38). It is significant to note that the Bible does not suggest that we give without expecting a return. Every command to give

comes with a promise. There are myriads of scriptures to this end. Clearly, God motivates generosity with promises of generous returns.

"'Yes' Jesus replied, 'and I assure you that everyone who has given up house or brothers or sisters or mother or father or children or property, for My sake and for the Good News, will receive now in return a hundred times as many houses, brothers, sisters, mothers, children, and property— along with persecution. And in the world to come that person will have eternal life'" (Mar 10:29, 30).

The harvest for sowing is not promised for the sweet by and by, it is promised for the here and now. The word used is *"now"*, and some Bible versions say, *"in this life"*. This promise is repeated throughout the scriptures. In fact, the Bible is so jam-packed with this idea that it would take far too many pages to list them all.

"Give generously, for your gifts will return to you later" (Ecc 11:1). Religion says that we are to give with the right motive, and then we are told that the right motive is not to expect anything in return.

Satan is so clever—he deals in half-truths. We certainly should give with the right motive—this is the half that is true. But what is the motivation given to us by God? He says, *"Give generously, for"* (the word *"for"* indicates motivation). And the motivation is, *"your gifts will return to you"*.

"Surely not! God would never motivate by appealing to self-interest." Really! Don't you think God knows us better than that? He knows only too well that nobody is completely selfless. We must admit that, more often than not, our very best shots are seldom altruistic. We may say that we are not doing it to be noticed by man, and that is commendable, but we cannot deny that we hope to be noticed by God. But not to worry— self-interest is no less laudable in His eyes.

Again and again, He appeals to our self-interest. Here's one: *"Today I have given you the choice between life and death, between blessings and curses. Now I call on heaven and earth to witness the choice you make. Oh, that you would choose life, so that you and your descendants might live!"* (Deut 30:19). Here He motivated them to choose correctly, so that they would have personal benefit. He appeals to their self-interest—their desire for life!

If you are thinking that the Old Testament doesn't apply to New Testament believers, then how about Jesus' ministry? *"Then Jesus said, 'Come to Me, all of you who are weary and carry heavy burdens, and I will give you rest'"* (Mat 11:28). Jesus tells us that we will get rest if we go to Him. Here, He appeals to our self-interest for resting.

...and He began to teach them. *"God blesses those who are poor and realize their need for Him, for the Kingdom of Heaven is theirs. God blesses those who mourn, for they will be comforted. God blesses those who are humble, for they will inherit the whole earth. God blesses those who hunger and thirst for justice, for they will be satisfied. God blesses those who are merciful, for they will be shown mercy. God blesses those whose hearts are pure, for they will see God. God blesses those who work for peace, for they will be called the children of God. God blesses those who are persecuted for doing right, for the Kingdom of Heaven is theirs"* (Mat 5:2-10).

This is better known as the "Sermon on the Mount". In it Jesus motivated us by appealing to our desire for personal benefit. Allow me to paraphrase:

God's Requirement	Motivation for Our Gain
Realise your need of Him	to obtain the Kingdom.
Mourn for your sins	to get God's comfort.
Humble yourself	to inherit the earth.
Hunger and thirst for justice	to be satisfied.
Be merciful	to receive mercy.
Have pure hearts	to see God.
Work for peace	to be a child of God.
Be persecuted	to have the Kingdom of Heaven.

This list could be very long indeed if we were to include the many scriptures along the lines of, *"And if you give even a cup of cold water to one of the least of My followers, you will surely be rewarded"* (Mat 10:42).

Although this is how God motivates us to part with our possessions, we should never lose sight of the fact that any giving done without love will not profit us. *"If I gave everything I have to the poor and even sacrificed my body, I could boast about it; but if I didn't love others, I would have gained nothing."* (1Cor 13:3) Love is key!

Principle no 2 – Expectation (faith)

Nobody can receive a miracle from God without somebody's expectation—it's called faith. As discussed earlier, even Jesus could do no good thing in Nazareth because of their unbelief. *"And it is impossible to please God without faith. Anyone who wants to come to Him must believe that God exists and that He rewards those who sincerely seek Him"* (Heb 11:6). Believing that He is God is not enough, God requires us to believe that He *"rewards"* those who sincerely seek Him.

From John 3:16 we saw that God didn't give His son without expecting a huge harvest of sons. In the same way, we should live in high expectation whenever we give. God creates with expectation, sows with expectation, speaks with expectation. Expectation should be at the top of our page, right next to love. It is how we activate the supernatural.

Sight operates in the dimension of the natural; faith operates in the dimension of the supernatural. As believers, this is where our strength lies. In this dimension the impossible becomes possible.

We are not earthly beings having a spiritual experience, we are spiritual beings having an earthly experience. And our earthly experience is brief by comparison to what awaits us on the other side.

We are not supposed to live our lives limited to our earning ability or business acumen. We are supposed to live spiritual lives with an unfair advantage! The earthly realm is far outranked by the spiritual realm—it is without limits—the miraculous is normal. This is what God intended for us in our everyday lives. We are not supposed to worry; we are supposed to live above earthly cares.

God puts such a high price on expectation (faith), that upon seeing it in Abraham, He accredited him with righteousness. Nowhere in scripture do we see God accrediting righteousness for any other personal virtue. He has never even accredited righteousness for piety or love. Though we know that anything done without love is worthless, it is nevertheless significant that God has such a high regard for expectation (faith).

Seeds need nourishment in order to germinate. Faith allows God to breathe His nourishment onto our seed. Without faith there will be no nourishment, and without nourishment there can be no harvest. It is not our seed that impresses God; it is our faith. Like epoxy glue, the two elements come in two separate tubes. Neither of these elements on their own have the power to glue anything together, but when combined, they form an unbreakable bond. Similarly, faith on its own without works is useless, and by the same token, works without faith are equally useless. The act of sowing is a work, that when combined with faith, results in a harvest!

God said that anything we give up for Him will come back to us thirty, sixty and one hundred-fold. To not expect a return for sowing, in the face of God's promise to give us a return, would be the same as not expecting to be saved in the face of God's promise to save us. The same principle of expectation applies to Seedtime and Harvest as applies to Salvation—it simply cannot happen without expectation. Amazingly, God wiped out all our sins for no other reason than that, upon hearing the gospel, we called on His name in expectation of receiving something from Him.

Without expectation	*With Expectation*
We can't get saved.	We get saved.
We can't exercise authority	We exercise authority

We can't get healed.	We get healed.
We can't get answers to prayer.	We get answers to prayer.
We can't prophesy	We prophesy
We can't work miracles	We work miracles.
We can't get a harvest	We get a harvest.

In the same way that our lack of expectation strips our prayers of power, our lack of expectation strips our seeds of the miracle of multiplication.

God's words are creative, because He is all powerful. By the same token, having become one with Him, our words are creative. What is our identity as believers? *"As he is, so are we in this world"* (I John 4:17).

Religion would have us believe that this verse is a command for us to strive to become like Him, but this is certainly not a command; it is a factual statement. We are already like Him! Our spirit man is no different to Him. *"We know that, when he shall appear, we shall be like him"* (I John 3:2). We might not realise it now, but when we eventually see Him, we are going to discover that we are precisely like Him.

Principle no 3 – God is our Source

"It's not important who does the planting, or who does the watering. What's important is that God makes the seed grow" (I Cor 3:7). The provision is all God's business—He is our source.

We should not expect a return from the person we are blessing with our giving. We should expect it from Jehovah Jirah, our provider. He alone is our source.

"Give your gifts in private, and your Father, who sees everything, will reward you" (Mat 6:4). The One who rewards, according to this verse, is our Father.

"And this same God who takes care of me will supply all your needs from His glorious riches, which have been given to us in Christ Jesus" (Phil 4:19). Though He may use men, it is from His riches in glory that He multiplies our seed.

No one is wealthy enough to impress God. He is infinitely wealthier than the wealthiest of the wealthy. When He gives out of His wealth, it does not impoverish Him. In the same way that there is no end to eternity, there is no end to His provisions.

Our city's newspaper headlines carried the story of gold teeth fillings miraculously appearing during John and Bev Sheasby's meetings held at our church some years ago. Good honest church people who did not attend these meetings were sceptical, saying that this phenomenon could not possibly be from God. After all, God would know better than to give gold teeth to the well-to-do while there are starving millions living in shanty towns. They obviously thought that God's supply of gold was limited. They could not see that He was simply responding with appreciation to John's message about the goodness of God. God was enjoying the truth being told about His love towards people and used gold to show us His appreciation!

A godly couple, who were sceptical of this phenomenon, came to my birthday party and got into conversation with a conservative Christian lady from a traditional church who had attended John's meetings. She had been blessed with a tooth of gold. She could hardly contain her excitement, taking it to be confirmation of His love for her. Elated, she literally bubbled with the excitement of telling her story. Although the sceptical couple left my party unmoved by her excitement, to their utter surprise, they woke the next morning to discover that they too had been blessed with gold fillings. Don't you just love God's sense of humour?

There is no limit to God's gold and wealth. And He sets no limit on the withdrawals we make from our heavenly bank account. Yet there are limits! Although God does not set them, we are not as kind to ourselves. It is we who limit the harvest by the quantity of seed we are prepared to sow. God doesn't need our money in heaven—there is nothing to spend it on there. We are the ones who need our seed to be in a place where rust and moth does not corrupt it—a place where it is divinely preserved and multiplied, ready to be withdrawn when required. It goes without saying that we can bless more people with divinely multiplied recourses, than we can with un-multiplied resources.

We sell our abilities on the labour market—it's how we earn a living. But sowing from our resources to reap from God's resources is altogether another matter. In being content with the world's system of eking out a living, we effectively reject the Kingdom's way of doing things, and in the process miss out on a life of unfair kingdom advantage. We may be God honouring in every respect, yet disappoint Him by failing to allow Him the pleasure of blessing us through His covenant of seedtime and harvest.

Despite Jesus describing the very kingdom of God as being *"seedtime and harvest"*, many refuse to accept this most vital of kingdom principles, relegating it to a freakish "prosperity cult". How sad to exclude oneself from a vital kingdom privilege—Jesus went to a lot of pain and trouble to obtain it for us. But as sad as it is to say, many forgo their kingdom privileges simply because it doesn't fit neatly into their particular religious paradigms.

Being independent—a self-made man, may sound heroic to some, but by leaving God's Kingdom process out of the equation, our material achievements are no different to the material achievements of unbelievers.

In the parable of the talents in Matthew 25, it is interesting to note that God did not test the three servants with holiness; He tested them with money. And then, He didn't judge them according to their piety; He judged them according to the profitability of their investments. He didn't test them with love or one of the other fruits of the Spirit; He tested them with hard "cash".

Similarly, He is testing you and me this very moment, and based on our obedience to this most vital of kingdom principles, we will one day be judged.

Laws that override other Laws

If we jump off a cliff, gravity ensures that we always fall downwards. As strong as this law is, there is another law that gives us immunity from the law of gravity. It's the law of lift. The aerodynamic shape of the leading edge of an aeroplane's wing causes a low pressure to form above it that has a stronger upward pull than the downward pull of gravity. A case of one law overriding another. In the same way, God's law of seedtime and harvest overrides the natural law of poverty and lack. The law of poverty says, "Keep everything you've got so that you don't become poorer"; while the law of seedtime and harvest says, "Give away what you have in order to reap a harvest."

Principle no 4 – Seed not Bread

We should not waste our breath praying for a harvest if we have not put seed in the ground. Without seed there simply will not be a harvest. God can multiply "little" seed, and He can multiply "much" seed, but He cannot multiply "no" seed. For a farmer to expect his fields to produce a harvest without planting seed would be insanity!

Jesus multiplied food for thousands on two separate occasions. He is God—why did He need fishes and loaves to multiply? Couldn't He have made bread and fish out of thin air? Even Jesus used bread and fishes as seed to obtain a greater harvest of bread and fishes. It's the way the Kingdom works.

Just as He cannot break His law to save us unless we call on His name, so He cannot break His law of seedtime to give us a harvest unless we have seed in the ground!

Now that is taking it a bit too far Deon. Isn't God omnipotent? Can't He do whatever He wants to, whenever He wants to? No, He can't! There are a number of things that God cannot do.

- He cannot break His word (Num 23:19)
- He cannot refuse to forgive you (1 John 1:9)
- He cannot refuse to save you (John 3:16)
- He cannot remember your sins (Jer 31:34)
- He cannot sin (1 Pet 1:16)
- He cannot do anything on this earth unless He has first revealed it to His prophets (Amos 3:7)
- He cannot lie (Num 23:19)
- He cannot usurp man's dominion of this earth (Gen 1:28)

- He cannot control our will. He respects the sovereign free will He gave us (Gen 1:28)
- He cannot do any good thing for us without somebody exerting faith (James 1:7)
- He cannot multiply our seed unless it is in the ground (2 Cor 9:10)

You might be thinking, "How dare you put God in a box?" Don't blame me, I didn't write these scriptures.

This doesn't mean that He is not capable of doing anything; it simply means that He won't use His omnipotence if it means losing His integrity. If He were to breach His integrity only once, He would no longer be holy, and He would have to bear that stain forever. He doesn't use His omnipotence to break covenant, He uses His omnipotence to fulfil covenant. His integrity (holiness) assures us that He will abide by His covenant.

Principle no 5 – Obedience

Satan would like us to believe that we should only give if we are able to take care of our own needs first. After all, how can we be expected to give when we can't even afford to feed our own children? Sounds right doesn't it? The problem with this thinking is that it is the world's wisdom. Again, God's way is precisely opposite. In the Kingdom, when we find ourselves in a financial fix, giving becomes even more imperative than when we are flush.

A mother had run out of food and was about to prepare one final meal for herself and her son, and then most likely starve to death. Just then, someone asked her for a meal. She had to decide, should she feed the stranger or her starving son with her last morsels? Common sense tells us that there is absolutely no contest; her first responsibility lies with her son. It is unreasonable to expect her to be thinking about giving at a time like this, right? Nobody would blame her for putting her precious son's needs ahead of a complete stranger's. Imagine the criticism she would have to face if she provided a meal for a stranger at the expense of her son's life?

Given these circumstances, what would you do? Would you feed your starving son, or risk him dying in order to feed a complete stranger? Let's face it, the whole world would support you if you chose to put your son's welfare first. But is that really the Kingdom's way? The Kingdom's way is to plant a seed when you are in need.

This is a true story. It is recorded in the 17th Chapter of I Kings. The mother in this story is the widow of Zarepheth, and the stranger is the prophet Elijah. She obediently gave the stranger her last meal. But the story doesn't end there. Her courageous sowing brought in a motherlode of harvests. From that day forward, her flour and olive oil kept multiplying. *"There was always enough flour and olive oil left in the containers, just as the LORD had promised through Elijah"* (I Kings 17:16). Imagine if she had taken the view that you don't give unless you have surplus enough to do so. God would have had to let her and her son starve to death.

The blessing didn't end there; it spilled over into other aspects of her and her son's lives. Later, when her son died, it was Elijah's prayers that raised him back to life. *"The LORD heard Elijah's prayer, and the life of the child returned, and he revived!"* (I Kings 17:22). If she had fed her son instead of the stranger, she would have lost her son later anyway. Her obedience to sow, saved her son on two separate occasions.

When God asks us to sow, He is not trying to get something from us; He is trying to get something to us. As much as He wants to bless us with a harvest, He cannot do so unless we have seed in the ground. For God to grant a harvest without a seed, He would have to violate His Covenant, and we know that He would never do that.

Any farmer worth his salt knows that you should only sow seed when conditions are conducive. Farmers are not likely to sow in times of extreme drought. Better to wait for conditions to improve than to waste precious seed. But again, God's way is different. I know of someone who obediently sowed in dry dusty sands right in the middle of a drought. Other farmers preserved their seed for better weather conditions. But despite good common sense, this farmer went ahead with his sowing, and guess what? He reaped a hundred times more than he put into the ground. The man's name was Isaac. *"A severe famine now struck the land….When Isaac planted his crops that year, he harvested a hundred times more grain than he planted, for the LORD blessed him. He became a very rich man, and his wealth continued to grow. He acquired so many flocks of sheep and goats, herds of cattle, and servants that the Philistines became jealous of him"* (Gen 26:1,12-14).

Should we sow in famine or in plenty? Common sense tells us that we should only sow when we are in plenty, but the Kingdom's way is to sow at all times, but more especially in times of famine. If Isaac had waited for good conditions before sowing, would He ever have become the wealthiest man on earth? Anybody can give in times of plenty. Bill Gates does; his annual giving runs into many billions of dollars. As good as this is, does it have the same impact as the widow's mite in God's economy?

Interestingly, Isaac didn't sow into the ministry—he sowed into his own business (farming) and enjoyed God's multiplication. Sowing is not restricted to religious institutions. Even God's original covenant with Adam of seed time and harvest had no religious connotations. Adam had nowhere to sow except into his own business and family, and we should do likewise. There are myriads of opportunities for sowing.

"He that observeth the wind shall not sow; and he that regardeth the clouds shall not reap" (Ecc 11:4). This verse deals with those who believe that they should not give when they are in lack. Clearly, without seed in the ground, they cannot expect to reap a harvest. Nowhere in scripture has God ever promised us a harvest without seed, so why waste time praying for one? He has however promised to provide seed to the sower, so a prayer asking for seed is a prayer that God can answer.

Seed and not Bread

"And God will generously provide all you need. Then you will always have everything you need and plenty left over to share with others. As the Scriptures say, 'They share freely and give generously to the poor. Their good deeds will be remembered forever.' For God is the One who provides seed for the farmer and then bread to eat. In the same way, He will provide and increase your resources and then produce a great harvest of generosity in you" (2 Cor 9:8-10).

If we are going to pray for our needs to be met without seed in the ground, we would be praying to the wind. According to this scripture, we should be praying for seed, not bread. Apple seed instead of apples. One large apple could at best feed one small person only once. On the other hand, one apple seed could feed multiplied thousands time and again. One seed could become an orchard with rows of apple trees laden with fruit every apple season, year after year. What we have in our pantry could either feed us or be multiplied in the hands of Jesus to feed many.

Seedtime and harvest of material things is God's idea. We are left without any doubt that the seed mentioned in the preceding scripture refers to material things. It says, "give generously to the poor". What do poor people need? Is it not material help?

In this scripture, Paul's teaching on material harvests for material sowing is not likened to a farmer by accident. Can you imagine a farmer sowing seed and then going on holiday at harvest time, because he doesn't think it is right to expect anything in return? A mindless notion! Of course, everybody knows that, after ploughing and sowing, farmers anxiously await their harvests with eager anticipation!

It sounds very pious to say that we are giving without expecting a return. It is what Satan would want us say. As long as we insist on taking this sanctimonious sounding line, Satan can keep God from establishing His covenant with us. (Deut 8:18). If we dare to teach others not to expect anything in return, we become a tool in Satan's hands, blocking God from establishing His covenant in the lives of others. Obviously, this is not something we should be doing—defying God is not at all clever!

God's answer to our lack

"Give freely and become more wealthy; be stingy and lose everything" (Prov 11:24). As usual, God's way does not make sense. We need to have the same seemingly nonsensical mentality as God in order to understand Him. God's ways are not our ways; they are much higher than our ways. They are always going to appear foolish to believers who have chosen not to live by them.

He commands the Israelites to march seven days around the walls of Jericho, and He tells Naaman to dip seven times in the river Jordan. It is nonsensical—it just doesn't add up! But the mighty fortified walls of Jericho would not have fallen, and Naaman would not have been healed of leprosy if they had not obeyed what must have seemed like sheer insanity. We have the benefit of hindsight, knowing how their obedience paid off. But they obeyed without the benefit of hindsight. Just as six times would not have brought the walls down, expecting a harvest without sowing seed would achieve nothing.

Oral Roberts' pioneering revelations were revolutionary to the church in his time. History shows that God chooses specific men to restore specific Kingdom principles at strategic times on His calendar. God chose Oral Roberts to lead the church back to the basics of faith in the 1940s, 50s and 60s. Many of his sermons are regarded as classics to this day. As a mass soul harvester, his name is ranked with DL Moody and Billy Graham. Nobody had performed as many miraculous healings in the history of the church. Nobody had built a more architecturally spectacular university without the benefit of resources. In today's money, he harvested billions of dollars by seed faith alone. His university has schooled many of the foremost Christian authors and leaders of our day. He stood head and shoulders above the faith giants of his time—a sort of modern-day Abraham.

Someone asked him what his greatest discovery about the Kingdom was, and then waited with bated breath for some deeply profound pearl of wisdom. The great man leaned forward and answered, "Sowing seed towards a specific result." Is that the best he could come up with? Surely such an enormously anointed leader should have discovered a deeper Bible truth than that! Besides, shouldn't he have sowed with a more altruistic motive? But had he not obediently sowed towards a specific result, his spiritual influence would not have amounted to more than a row of beans.

God does not put sickness, pain, poverty or lack on us to see how well we endure trials. But He does test our faith. He wants to know what we will do with our assets. He is more interested in our faith than in our church attendance. Faith is demonstrated in obedience to His words. The choice is simple. Do we use what's in our wallets as seed or as bread? Herein lies the test!

God is waiting on the other side of our obedience with a miracle. Nothing we do in obedience goes unrewarded.

It's a Matter of Proportions

"Give, and you will receive. Your gift will return to you in full—pressed down, shaken together to make room for more, running over, and poured into your lap. The amount you give will determine the amount you get back" (Luke 6:38).

It is all about proportions. God can only multiply what we have sown. The amount sown determines the amount reaped. It stands to reason that a wheat farmer who sows ten fields will harvest more than a wheat farmer who sows one field, and a farmer who sows nothing, will have nothing to harvest.

Why don't we always reap in practise? In the Kingdom, nothing happens without emphatic faith. Faith says, "I have what was promised. I don't need to wait and see if it actually materialises. God's word and my faith in it, is all the evidence I need". Faith believes that our harvest is a done deal. It was this kind of faith that impressed Jesus—the same kind of faith that the Centurion expressed when he asked Jesus to pray for his servant. On the other hand, the religious view, that we are to give without expecting a return, does not require faith to bring about results, and without faith it is impossible to please God.

Notice that we receive in direct proportion to what we have given. *"The amount you give will determine the amount you get back"* (Luke 6:38). Giving a little will return a little. Giving nothing will return nothing, and not even God can ignore this law. By the way, a little can be a lot, as in the case of the widow's mite. It's all relative.

What about Philippians 4:19: *"And this same God who takes care of me will supply all your needs from His glorious riches, which have been given to us in Christ Jesus."*

This verse is often quoted without taking the trouble to understand its context. We are wasting our breath on this scripture, unless of course, we have seed in the ground. The preceding verses speak of the faithful giving of the Philippians. The promise of Philippians 4:19 only applies to those who, like the Philippians, have been faithfully giving. For God to give us a harvest when there is no seed in the ground, He would have to contravene His covenant, and we know that that is not going to happen. Even for Him to give us a harvest by any measure other than the measure of our sowing, would make Him a covenant-breaker. God will never violate His word to make an exception for anyone.

God's Antidote for Greed

This principle seems so worldly, doesn't it? Pay God a fee to get rich. Doesn't it appear as though this would suit greedy people? They can feed their greed and get greedier, right? Seems wrong doesn't it? That's because it is wrong! Greedy people may part with their money once, but they will do it with reluctance, thereby forfeiting the reward promised to the cheerful giver.

If everything we own already belongs to God, why are we holding onto it so tightly? We shouldn't be asking Him how much we should give; we should be asking Him how much we should keep. Greedy people are simply unable to embrace the principle of liberality. It runs contrary to greed.

There are four reasons for our reluctance to give: ignorance; fear; selfishness and greed. All totally ungodly reasons.

- Ignorance—we have not discovered the Kingdom's way of doing things.
- Fear—we're not entirely convinced that we can trust God to do what He said He would.
- Selfishness—we live our lives unto ourselves.
- Greed—we want all we can get without giving anything away.

How does God get us to overcome these ills? He sets before us His plan of seedtime and harvest. Greed simply cannot survive the cycle of seedtime and harvest. Nobody can be greedy and generous at the same time.

God has a plan to finance the last push to reach lost souls for the kingdom before Jesus returns. His plan is seedtime and harvest. We simply cannot earn enough to finance the promised end-time harvest of souls—meagre earnings are not enough. With our limited resources, too many souls will remain unreached, doomed to a Christless eternity. Part of our earnings needs to be seed, not bread. The gospel needs something bigger than our resources; it needs multiplication—the harvest that comes from diligent sowing.

The principle of seedtime and harvest is a never-ending cycle. We ought always to use part of our harvest to sow for an even bigger harvest. It's how we keep the cycle turning. Generosity begets generously.

The DNA of Seed

"And God said, Let the earth bring forth grass, the herb yielding seed, and the fruit tree yielding fruit after his kind, whose seed is in itself, upon the earth: and it was so" (Gen 1:11). When we sow tomato seeds, we reap tomatoes, and when we sow orange seeds, we reap oranges. When we sow kindness, we reap kindness and when we sow love, we reap love. God ordained that everything will produce after its kind.

For the most part, bank currency has no value of its own; it's just little slips of printed paper. It's the effort that we put into obtaining these little pieces of paper that give them value. Our money represents our time and skills—effort exerted in blood, sweat and tears. To an accountant, it represents time spent auditing, and to a motor mechanic, it represents time spent fixing cars.

Money can represent anything—it has no DNA. When we sow money, we can give it any DNA we please, so that it can produce after its kind. We give it its DNA by stating what kind of seed it is. If we are sowing for a car, we can name it car seed, if we are sowing for a job, we can name it job seed, and if we are sowing for somebody's salvation, we can name it salvation seed.

"Cornelius stared at him in terror. 'What is it, sir?' he asked the angel. And the angel replied, 'Your prayers and gifts to the poor have been received by God as an offering!'" (Act 10:4). The result of Cornelius' seed was that he and his whole house received salvation.

What is your need? Give a name to the money you are sowing, so that it can produce what you want to harvest. It will produce after its kind.

Testimony

On a personal note, my Aunt Nola looked after their family finances. Her husband, Claude, was in the ministry. They were desperately poor. The church was tiny and on the wrong side of town. It couldn't afford to pay them anything close to a liveable wage. Their children had to attend church in their school uniforms, because they couldn't afford smart clothes.

Though in desperate straits, they chose to scrimp and scrape and do without rather than skip a single tithe. They were totally convinced that the law of seedtime and harvest would eventually pay off. It took years of struggle, but eventually the blessings started going their way. When this happened, they didn't splurge out on themselves, they simply doubled up their giving. That's when the momentum of the blessings picked up. When they moved their giving up to 30%, the blessings just got bigger and better, so they moved their giving up to 40%. Not content with this level, they continued ratcheting it up in stages until their giving reached 90% of their wages. This left them with only 10% to live on, but with their harvest streaming in, they lacked nothing. In fact, by this time they were so blessed that they were taking regular overseas holidays in 5-star luxury and were regular round-the-world travellers on the QE2.

Then they decided that if they could trust God with 90% of their income, they might as well trust Him with 100%. They decided to tell the church to stop paying them altogether. I was the church treasurer at the time. Instead of taking a salary, every month they would simply hand me a list of all the people and organisations they wanted to bless out of what they would normally have gotten as salary. Their entire salary became a blessing to others. No longer receiving any compensation whatsoever for their diligent labours. But the blessings just kept rolling in—way more than they could ever have earned.

Property deals and more blessings just kept chasing them down. Almost daily, Aunty Nola would experience new financial miracles, like the time she went to her wardrobe to get dressed. She looked at her more than ample assortment of outfits and said, "Lord, wouldn't it be nice to have a new set of clothes". No sooner had the words left her mouth than the phone rang and a voice on the other end said, "I own a boutique and will be running a sale from tomorrow. Would you like to come around and pick out six new outfits for yourself free of charge before they go on sale?" And so, the blessings just kept rolling in.

Sowers have big expectations. Without mentioning it to anyone, Aunty Nola asked the Lord to give her family a holiday in Hawaii. Some believers may have a problem with such boldness—why Hawaii, why not Durban or somewhere less extravagant?

Then out of the blue, a lady who wasn't a member of our church, but had attended her ladies' meetings, gave her a large sum of money specifically for her to take her family on holiday. It was enough for Hawaii. Aunty Nola said that she felt that she couldn't receive the kind offer because one of her sons, Geoff, was in his first year, serving a three-year term of army conscription on the Angolan border. "How could I enjoy the tropical delights of Waikiki Beach while my son eats baked beans and bully beef and sleeps on the ground?" she thought. Then the Lord replied, "I don't have problems, I only have plans." So, she wrote to the military asking them to grant her son all the leave that would become due to him over the next three years. She wanted it all in one stretch for a family holiday in Hawaii. Anybody who knows the military knows that this is a daft request. Civilian employers wouldn't entertain such an outlandish request, let alone the military.

As expected, her request was refused outright and with contempt, but army procedure required the officer to pass on all correspondence to the next level of command. Again, the request was instantly turned down without giving it so much as a second thought, and again it was passed on to the next level of command and naturally turned down once again.

At this point most people would have given up believing for it. They would probably say, "It's not God's will to answer this prayer" or "Surely this was expecting a bit much from the military? Most folk would gasp at her audacity, saying, "How dare she have the nerve to expect God to go along with such outrageousness?" But not Aunty Nola—she just doggedly hung onto the words that the Lord had given her, "I don't have problems, I only have plans". Against all odds, she persisted to believe that Geoff would be granted the equivalent of three years leave in advance. As you can imagine, Geoff thought his mother had lost her marbles.

As with all correspondence on the border, the letter was passed on to military HQ in Pretoria. The next thing, Geoff was summoned to appear before the Battalion Commander. With fear and trepidation, he made his way to the commander's office, wondering what he had done wrong to warrant such an order. He found the Commander at his desk looking profoundly perplexed, shaking his head in disbelief. He said, "Never in all my years as a military man, have I ever heard anything as crazy as this." Instead of a reprimand, he handed Geoff a letter from HQ granting him all the leave that would become due to him over the next three years for the purpose of a holiday in Hawaii.

Never before had anyone been granted special leave to go to any beach, let alone Hawaii! Dumb struck, the Commander blurted out: "What has become of the military?" This was a far cry from the disciplined armed service he thought he knew.

Seed faith people are no different to others—just ordinary people like you and me. But what makes them different is that they have discovered how to make withdrawals from their heavenly bank account, where rust and moth does not corrupt.

The first leg of their journey was to New York, then Los Angeles and finally Honolulu. They arrived in New York only to discover that JFK airport was in the middle of a strike. This caused their connecting flight to be delayed by three hours. After having travelled so far, they could do without added frustrations!

While waiting, the Lord prompted Aunty Nola to ask the airways lady behind the counter if she could help them with booking accommodation in Hawaii. The lady said that she was unable to help, but that her boss' plane had just touched down. He was returning from Hawaii, maybe he could advise them.

They were introduced to him, and it just so happened that he owned a luxury condominium right on Waikiki beach—the choicest of spots—beyond their wildest dreams! The man graciously let them stay in his condominium. Such a chance meeting would never have taken place if their flight had not been delayed. God had gone before them, marshalling mighty airlines and a luxury condominium owner to slot in with the plans of a simple seed sower.

Without a salary or a pension in their old age, they continue to live like royalty, spending six months a year abroad. Wherever they go, their focus is on helping others in word and deed. They attract the needy like a magnet, saving some on the brink of suicide; supporting others materially; encouraging others; prophesying to some; leading the lost to salvation and so on. Their lives overflow with generosity to hurting and needy people, touching many with the love of Jesus. In the last fifty years they have owned many cars but have only sold one. The rest were all given away.

These accounts are just some of the many incidents of extreme favour in the lives of this blessed couple—a brief glimpse into the lives of faithful seed sowers. They're not nervous about giving. Why would they be? More than fifty years of living by the miracle of seedtime and harvest would be more than enough to assure anybody, wouldn't you say?

In reading their story, do not lose sight of the fact that it all began in abject poverty with nothing but a big God, a tiny seed and a determination to sow it with love, even when it really hurt.

Tithing is another subject altogether and is not covered in this book. The liberality and freedom of joyful seedtime and harvest far out classes compulsory giving.

We may be able to give a persuasive argument as to why we believe that seedtime and harvest is not for modern day believers. As convincing as we may be, one thing is certain, we will never be able to convince Uncle Claude and Aunty Nola!

Martin Luther's Statement

"Satan will use poverty and tyrants to prevent the spreading of the gospel."

The spreading of the Gospel needs more funding than our meagre resources, it needs the harvest from diligent sowing.

Covenant

Through God's covenant with Abraham, all believers are blessed. In it, there is no mention of seedtime and harvest. How do we reconcile what seems to be a contradiction between Abraham's covenant and the covenant of seed time and harvest?

In Abraham's covenant we are not blessed for planting seeds; we are blessed purely because we have been grafted into Abraham's family through Jesus. Many would say that Abraham was blessed for his onetime tithe to Melchizedek. But that is not why he was counted righteous. It happened before he met Melchizedek. He was blessed for one reason and one reason only—He believed God for the impossible. And that was enough for God to count his faith for righteousness.

We simply cannot earn the right to Abraham's blessings—besides, there is no need for that—it's already ours, and it came to us purely by grace. Church attendance, tithing, praying, fasting, good deeds, church leadership, uprightness and integrity, as good as all of these are, they cannot trigger grace—grace is not something that can be earned.

Abraham was a sinful man. He went so far as to deny that he was married to his wife, Sarah, allowing others to molest her in order to get himself out of a fix. How despicable is that? He didn't get the blessing because he deserved it, he got it purely for believing what God had promised. And that's how we get it too—by faith in God's word alone.

"Seedtime and harvest" should not be confused with "tithing". With seed time and harvest, we co-operate with God by sowing into our own businesses, investments, families, relationships, churches, mission fields, the poor, orphans, widows and anywhere else He may direct us.

Seed is not necessarily money—it could be actual seed if you are a farmer, or it could be the word of God if you are a preacher. Jesus described the word of God as seed. The Bible is a whole bag of seed ready for us to scatter. We scatter Bible seed when we declare His words into existence by faith—speaking things that be not as though they are.

The reason for our present condition, whether good or bad, can often be traced back to our past sowing. If we are wondering why we have harvested hatred, perhaps we will find the answer in the hatred we have sown. If we have harvested criticism, it is likely that we have sown criticism. If we have harvested honour, it is likely that we have honoured others.

"Now you are taking this too far Deon", you may be thinking. Well then consider these outcomes: We harvest emphysema and cancer when we sow chain smoking; cirrhosis of the liver when we sow alcoholism; education when we sow studying; a smile when we sow a smile; love when we sow love; friendship when we sow friendship. We cannot escape seedtime and harvest—everything that we undertake is a seed, and every seed has a harvest. *"Be not deceived; God is not mocked: for whatsoever a man soweth, that shall he also reap"* (Gal 6:7).

Some Christians feel manipulated by ministries who use the teaching of seedtime and harvest to extract finances from them, making all kinds of questionable promises. Use discernment before you jump in with your cheque book. Be very wary whenever guilt is used to motivate giving. Unless you have a clear leading from God, sowing into an institution at the expense of your family is ungodly.

Isaac's farming business flourished one hundred-fold when he sowed directly into the ground. The principle of Seedtime and Harvest is all embracing—not restricted to church fund raising. The best advice I can give, is to be guided by the Spirit.

There is no greater motivation for giving than in the life of Jesus. He gave His life to save a bunch of scallywags of the likes of you and me. It wasn't nails that held Jesus to the cross; it was His love for us. If we can grasp the gravity of His love, we will find ourselves loving others more—not in words alone, but in deeds of kindness—His liberality begetting our liberality. If we, in our raggedy state, were so graciously accepted by God, then surely, the least we can do is to be gracious to others regardless of their raggediness.

We ought never to measure our giving with a calculator—better to measure it with love and compassion!

God's Character

Some Christians love to speak about looking into the eyes of Jesus. In Him they find forgiveness, unconditional love and acceptance. But their concept of God the Father's eyes is often very different to those of Jesus'. Somehow, they would feel less than worthy to look into His face. He is often depicted as stern and severe. Some even visualise Him holding a bolt of lightning like a javelin, ready to strike anybody daring to step out of line.

Seeing that no-one has actually seen the Father, and that everybody seems to have a different idea of Him, how in the world can we be sure that our concept of Him is right? After all, God is high and lifted up, isn't He? Maybe mortals are not even supposed to know what He is like.

Is it even possible to know His character and personality? We most certainly can! We have been given a full description of him. This is what Jesus had to say on the subject, *"Anyone who has seen Me has seen the Father! So why are you asking Me to show Him to you?"* (John 14:9). Every Bible description of Jesus is a perfect description of our loving Father. If Jesus is loving, forgiving, kind, compassionate, merciful and caring, then so is our Father. In fact, Jesus is the exact image and likeness of the Father (John 1:1; 2 Cor 3:17, 4:6; Col 1:15; Heb 1:3). Perfectly mirrored in Jesus. And nobody is more completely described in scripture than Jesus.

We have come to see the Father as one who is strict and intolerant of our less than perfect way of living, but the Bible's description of Him is very different. It says that He will not even crush a bruised reed. He works gently with bruised egos and hurting souls—never harsh with offenders.

Each of us come to different conclusions about who God the Father is and end up serving the image we have created of Him. If our perceptions of Him do not align with the Bible description of Jesus, our mis-perceptions will misdirect our relationships. Some feel obliged to tippy toe around Him as if in a diplomatic minefield. Others have learnt that they can be themselves while at home with the One who loves having His toddlers around. Some have an oppressive relationship, while others enjoy a romance made in heaven. Sadly, for some, the thought of intimacy is most unlikely.

Here are some typical relationship destroying lies: God is angry with us; punishing us; hurting us to teach us a lesson; not answering our prayers until we get our lives straightened out; putting sickness on us to draw us closer to Him; exercising His sovereignty over us; or the Lord gives and the Lord takes away. As already stated, any concept of God the Father that is not true of the compassionate Jesus described in the Bible, is nothing but a blatant lie!

We come to these distorted conclusions, because we are eating the fruit of the knowledge of good and evil. From that perspective, we are likely to make warped conclusions regarding His nature and character. The portrait that we paint of our Father becomes an unfortunate caricature with disproportionate features—distorting His infinite goodness, making Him out to be a monstrous ogre. Fortunately, nothing can be further from the truth!

In getting His character wrong, we are likely to attribute the woes of this world to God. We'll say that He is responsible for the Planet's catastrophes. They are His doing, His discipline, His punishment, His moulding of our characters, His display of love for us, etc. It is not unusual to hear these trite Christianese explanations expressed. But no matter how religious sounding they may be, lies are plain and simply lies!

Insurance companies call storm damage, an act of God. It would be more accurate to call it an act of nature. Mother Nature is not married to Father God—they are not even distant cousins—how could they be? She is no more than a figment of our imagination. Blaming nature on God causes people to believe a lie about His loving character. No matter how we look at it, our knowledge of good and evil will have us placing the blame for the world's ills on an innocent God, and in doing so, we will be letting a guilty devil off the hook. We do this in all innocence, but misinformation remains misinformation, no matter how innocent surmised!

Many unsaved people reason that, if there is a God, He must be in charge of the world. And if so, He is responsible for all the chaos, hurts and miseries. The picture they form of Him, although completely false, is the reason they give for not wanting to commit their lives to Him. With such distorted impressions of His gracious nature, who can blame them?

Even saved people reason that if their prayers go unanswered, it must be for some divine reason like, "God knows best." Again, He gets the blame. Such distortions of Him cause many to conclude that He cannot be taken at His word. They say He must have had a good reason like, we failed to live holy enough to be blessed. Unfortunately, they don't consider the myriad of other possibilities, such as having failed to exercise decisive divine authority. But then again, if they aren't convinced of their authority, they are going to be looking for someone else to carry the can for their faith failures. Just blame God—He is not one to defend Himself.

God's character is not meant to be a mystery—every book of the Bible reveals something of who He is. Through the spectrum of the life of Jesus, we get a precise picture of how loving, caring and compassionate God the Father is. Whatever conclusions we have come to regarding God's character, unless they square up with the character of Jesus, they are plain and simply defamatory! When people defame the character of others, they are sued in a court of law. But we think nothing of defaming God's character with all kinds of Christianese platitudes that have nothing in the world to do with Christianity.

There is no getting around it; if our ideas of God the Father are in any way contrary to the Jesus of the Bible, they are plain and simply wrong, period!

The death of Jesus reveals so much about the Father's heart. It speaks volumes of His loving nature. It seems there is no end to the lengths that He will go to in order to show us the extent of His love. A greater and purer love is simply not possible, not even in our wildest imaginations. His love is outrageous! How do we explain it? He is love struck with undeserving mortals and none of their sins are too terrible to block His love for them.

We all know that, for every denomination, there is a denominational slant, and they can't all be right. Either God the Father is like Jesus or our conclusions are offbeat! We do well to examine the picture that our particular religious group has given of Him.

God the Father looks like Jesus:

- Jesus set the oppressed free, because that is what the Father wants.
- Jesus healed the sick, because the Father wants us well.
- Jesus spoke words of life, because they are the Father's words.
- Jesus loved those who hated Him, because the Father loves those who hate Him.

- Jesus forgave sin, because the Father forgives sin.
- Jesus had compassion for wounded humanity, because the Father has compassion for wounded humanity.
- Jesus went to the cross to save us, because the Father loves us.
- Jesus draws us into His intimate embrace, because the Father is passionately in love with us.

God's Holiness

We often hear that God is gracious to us, because He is a gentleman. That He is a gentleman is certainly not in dispute, but maybe there is another reason for His graciousness. Maybe it has something to do with who He inherently is. He is holy and therefore His integrity is scrupulous! This assures us that He will never go back on His word. Holiness is not some godly status, like a doctor would use the letters PhD behind his name. It's a state of absolute unblemishable integrity that sets Him apart. He is separate and different!

By reason of His faultless integrity, He is trustworthy, incapable of breaking His word. Every promise can be relied upon to be fulfilled to the enth degree. If He had reserved the right to annul a contract, renege on a promise or rescind a covenant, He would no longer be able to claim to be faultless; He would have a chink in His armour; vulnerable to being overthrown.

Of course, none of this is remotely possible—His integrity is unquestionably flawless! It is His uncompromising holiness that secures His position as everlasting emperor of the entire universe. He doesn't make an attempt to be flawless; He is plain and simply incapable of anything less! As a holy God, He doesn't keep His word because He feels

He must; He just doesn't have the evil capacity within Himself to do otherwise!

You might be saying, "Now wait a minute Deon, you can't put God in a box!" Well, if you're suggesting that His sovereignty allows Him to lie, then you are inferring that He is untrustworthy, and that would make Him unholy. Let's face it, only fools would stake their lives on the promises of an unholy god. If that was true, none of His words and none of His promises would be worth the paper they are written on! Who would be foolish enough to entrust their lives to a liar? If this was so, we would all be in a whole heap of trouble! How could we ever be certain that we are really saved? How could we be sure that we will make it to heaven? If we cannot rely upon one of His promises, why on earth would we be so foolish as to believe the rest of them?

This kind of uncertainty would make us all a bunch of sorry individuals, living in a tentative hope—no better off than la-la-land! If we could not be sure that He is entirely dependable, how could we ever know where we stand with Him? Why would anybody forgo the indulgence of worldly pleasures for the sake of chasing the wind? Nothing but false claims, empty promises and misleading myths.

If He could change His mind willie-nillie, depending on His mood, He could be a loving Father one minute and a monsterous thug the next. It sounds more like the character of that pseudo god, the bogus one who goes by the reputation of a trickster, thief and murderer!

Thankfully, our God's character is one of rock-solid reliability, unshakable dependability and unquestionable integrity—a position that is forever incontestable. In a word, He is holy, a concept beyond the grasp of mortals.

One thing is certain: We can always count on Him. There is no limit to His integrity; no breaking point to His trustworthiness; His honesty is simply not for sale. Once He has said something, it is irrefutably certain!

He is bound by every word that leaves His mouth—His words are as immaculate as His character!

In a court of law, witnesses are asked to place their hands on a Bible and to swear to tell the truth, the whole truth and nothing but the truth, so help me God. No other book is as reliable!

At the precise moment of God's utterances, His words are instantly legally binding upon all parties concerned, and that includes Himself. He is not a man that He should lie. Not ever! Never, never, never! Either your future is secure in this knowledge, or you might as well indulge your sinful fantasies and make the best of a brief life to offset an awaiting catastrophic eternity. If it's okay for Him to break His word, then it's okay for you to break yours. But if He is holy, then His word is His bond, always and without exception!

To base one's future on His holy reputation, is to know without a shadow of doubt that He will honour every promise He has ever made. When He gave Adam sovereign dominion, He excluded Himself from interfering with his decisions. Adam foolishly squandered mankind's dominion, and because God, as almighty as He is, had no say over Adam's decisions, He could not use His sovereignty to stop Adam's folly.

When Adam traded mankind's dominion for the knowledge of good and evil, he sold us up the creek without a paddle. What a travesty! Because sovereign man had gotten himself and his descendants into this mess, only sovereign man could get themselves out of it. As much as God would have loved to step in and fix the problem for us, He did not have the legality to do so—it was within sovereign mankind's dominion. That left the problem in mankind's hands. But let's face it, mankind is flawed, lacking the necessary holy credentials to enter Satan's realm, wrestle man's rightful dominion from him, and survive the quest.

This was a task that had to be accomplished by a holy man; not a holy God. But in the next four thousand years, not one man was found to be holy. Not even great men like Noah, Moses, Abraham, David or Daniel. This placed man in a predicament. Somebody would have to enter Satan's realm, retrieve dominion, and have the holiness to leave there with his life intact. If Satan could find any sin in his life, he would have the legal right to keep him imprisoned.

As usual, God had a plan. But in not having sovereignty over man's domain, He lacked the necessary credentials to complete the task on man's behalf. So, to obtain them, He commissioned His Son to become a man, thus gaining a legal right to wrest man's dominion back from Satan's grasp. In His Son, He would have a perfect man to carry out the task. In becoming the Son of Man, Jesus obtained mankind's credentials, allowing Him to accomplish the task on mankind's behalf. He could enter Satan's realm and retrieve Adam's lost dominion. Interestingly, although Jesus was perfectly entitled to refer to Himself as the Son of God, He repeatedly referred to himself as the Son of Man, thus affirming His human identity. It was this that gave Him the necessary credentials to complete the task on man's behalf.

When Jesus died, He entered Satan's realm, bearing the sin of the world. Satan was convinced that he had scuppered God's plan. He had the son of God just where he wanted Him—ready to see Him fry. Nobody else had entered there with a fraction of the sin that He carried, though none of His own, and survived to tell the story. Satan was convinced that this gave him a legal right to keep the Son of God imprisoned. But to his dismay, he could not get any criminal charges against Him to stick. Jesus' personal perfection gave Him the legal right to leave hell unscathed, and when He left, He did not leave empty-handed. He brought mankind's dominion with Him. Now, in possession of mankind's dominion, He offers to restore it to any of us who would simply receive it by believing in the Son of God and calling on His name.

Born Again

"Jesus replied, 'I tell you the truth, unless you are born again, you cannot see the Kingdom of God'" (John 3:3).

Nicodemus' interest in meeting with Jesus wasn't to find out how to go to heaven, but rather to find out how the Messiah intended setting up His Kingdom on earth—how He intended ruling the world from Jerusalem. He wanted to be a part of the Messiah's government. We know this because the Jews of his day were expecting a Messiah to overthrow their Roman oppressors and set up a universal kingdom in Jerusalem. If we misunderstand his enquiry, we will misunderstand Jesus' answer. Was Jesus explaining the way to get to heaven when He said, *"You must be born again"*? Sure, we know that being born again is the only requirement for entering heaven, but that wasn't Nicodemus' interest, and Jesus knew it.

In telling Nicodemus that he must be born again, Jesus was explaining the way for him and for anybody else to reign on Planet Earth. Our reign on Earth doesn't start when we reach some level of spiritual maturity. No, it starts the precise moment we are born again. The one and only credential for reigning in life is rebirth—nothing else! Not holiness; not maturity; not sinlessness; not servanthood; not humility; not prayer; not fasting! As good as all of these are, it is rebirth alone that qualifies us to enter the

Kingdom and to reign as kings. Unless we know our Royal standing, we won't reign in life. Do we really know our identity as sons and daughters of the Most-High and our purpose as kings?

What a crying shame it is to see good honest godly people deferring their reign to a future date when they believe they will be holy enough. Or worse still, deferring it to when they get to heaven. In saying that our authority depends on our personal state of holiness, we are saying that Jesus' blood is not potent enough to make us entirely righteous.

Either we got our salvation by His blood or by personal holiness. We must decide. If by personal holiness, then we are all in big trouble, lost and miserable. Although we have been made perfect in God's eyes, we are certainly not perfect in a practical sense—our behaviour is in the process of being sanctified. No one in the history of mankind has ever reached a point where no further sanctification is necessary.

If, as some might say, we can only operate in authority from a position of holiness, then all are disqualified. Thank God this is not so. We do not carry our résumés of religious achievements; we carry His résumé of achievements. We have been divinely deputised to wield divine authority in the same way Jesus did.

Denominationally-prescribed levels of holiness are not what holiness is. As dreadful as sin is, the blood of Jesus is potent enough to take care of it. We operate in Kingdom authority by way of our "child of God" identity. We will never become more qualified than we were on the day we were born again. Jesus made it crystal clear that our Kingdom reign is based upon rebirth. He never so much as hinted that it hinges on behavioural holiness.

When He rules in our lives, His word is more believable than physical reality. So, when the doctor says that you are going to die, and God says that by Jesus' stripes you were healed, you must decide whose word you are going to believe, the doctor's or God's. You can't choose both. After all, they are completely opposite. Does the doctor's word count for more than God's? Both the doctor's and God's words are reliable. By accepting that God's word has the last say on the matter, you will be healed, but in taking the doctor's word as final, there is no doubt about it, you will die!

When God is allowed to rule, His word is more believable than the limiting words of small thinking mentors. Sadly, with small thinking, many find themselves confined to small reigning. We have to decide whether our school teacher's denigrating words, that we would never amount to anything, are more believable than God's. He said that we are more than conquerors, and that we can do all things through Christ who strengthens us. One thing is certain, if we believe her words more than God's, we can count on them being fulfilled—we will never amount to anything!

His word is more believable than the limitations our occupations have placed on our earning capacity. He said that with His wisdom we don't only get life, we get riches and honour (Prov 3:16). Are you going to allow your salary to be more convincing than His promise to prosper you? If you do so, you can be sure that you will stay poor. Of course, poverty is relative. Depending on your social standing, you could be poor with a seven-figure income.

His Kingdom on earth exists wherever believers allow Him to rule. God does not rule where the doctor, the teacher or the boss is more convincing than Him. You may say that He rules because you have chosen a chaste lifestyle and don't participate in worldly pleasures. But, don't be deceived. Unless you have given His word precedence over your physical, mental and material world, you are still living on the fringes of the Kingdom, vulnerable to Satan's trickery. That doesn't mean that you are not going to heaven, it simply means that you have chosen to live outside of the Kingdom's privileged way of life. God didn't rapture you when you were born again, nor did He tell you to endure sickness and lack until you die. He assigned you to reign over life's challenges until the day He comes. The Bible is clear: It says that in this life we would have many troubles, but that's not where it ends. It goes on to say that God would rescue us out of them all (Psalm 34:19). All He requires is our faith.

Can we walk totally committed to the Kingdom in every area of our lives? I have yet to meet such an individual. On our journey, we learn to draw ever greater amounts of God's faith from within us. His faith was deposited there at the precise moment of our rebirth (Rom 12:3).

Although God wants us to enjoy the royal privileges of His Kingdom in the here and now, too many receive eternal life, but fail to step through the palace doors to live as kings on earth. Outside of the palace, we are in Satan's territory—open to his harassment. Many put up with conflict, sickness, lack, disunity, failure, hurts, offenses and unhappiness, oblivious to the abundant provisions available to them. For them the joy of the Lord is only sung about on Sundays, but never actually experienced Monday through Saturday. Their churches may have convinced them that pain and suffering will be worth it all when we eventually see Jesus. How sad! God has done all He can to convince us to step into His Kingdom and to indulge in its treasures. Isn't it strange? It seems easier for Him to convince us to accept peace, joy and love in the life hereafter, than to accept them in the here and now! We should not be deferring God's favour to anther life. The doors to the palatial courts of our Daddy's Kingdom have been flung wide open. The invitation is out—walk right in! It is a place where our every action and word bear His authority. A place where we are inspired, uplifted, encouraged, guided and equipped to lead overcoming and fulfilled lives. It is all available to us for immediate use in the here and now!

Sonship

God's plan of salvation is not a matter of making bad people good. His plan is to give birth to sons.

What is sin? Sin is missing the mark. What is the mark? The mark is sonship! God's blueprint for mankind is sonship. How do we miss sonship? We don't grasp the fact that we are like Him. To live at any level less than sonship, is what sin is.

We can be so preoccupied with fixing the symptoms—the manifestations instead of the cause. Fighting sin is like treating cancer with a Band-Aid. The reason for our powerlessness is that we believe ourselves to be mere men. Mere men do not have the capacity to deal with sin effectively. God does not have this problem, nor do those of His kids who have discovered the implication of being His sons.

We all know that we were not saved by works and therefore cannot stay saved by works. Seeing that we were rebirthed despite our behaviour, it is obvious that we cannot be un-birthed because of our behaviour. We are sons for an entirely different reason. We are new creations, created in the image of the Father who gave us birth. Our sonship is our godlikeness. If we don't recognise our godlikeness, how closely we take after our heavenly Dad, we will miss our divine destiny and family privileges. I could have used the word Christlikeness instead of godlikeness, but Christlikeness is so often used to describe a form of Christian behaviour. This is not what I am referring to here. Our behaviour, whether good or bad, does not have a bearing on the fact that our spirit man is godlike.

God's love for us is not in response to something that we did or failed to do. Sin is not the issue. Sonship is the issue!

Why is it important to acknowledge our sonship? It is the very foundation of our faith. Either we base our good standing with our heavenly Father upon our spiritual rebirth, or upon our Christian performance! Some have hedged their bets by building their relationship with God on both foundations, and then wonder why their structure is so shaky. It is guaranteed, our personal performance will let us down! Anything built on wonky foundations eventually collapses. A relationship predicated upon the holiness of our living, is precarious, unstable and sure to crumble! These frail structures require on-going maintenance and propping up with all kinds of self-blame and shame.

Many Bible teachers warn us against the dangers of religion's dead works, and then proceed to teach us a different, yet equally dangerous set of dead works. Without a revelation of our godly identity, we are always going to misconstrue biblical descriptions of ourselves, as victors and conquerors, to be commandments to try to be victors and conquerors. With this mindset, we misconstrue descriptions of ourselves as victorious believers, to be lofty ideals that can hardly be attained by mortals. This kind of confusion has sent many a sincere believer on a wild goose chase. Such striving is as futile as trying to grasp the wind!

Take Galatians 5:22, 23 as an example. *"But the Holy Spirit produces this kind of fruit in our lives: love, joy, peace, patience, kindness, goodness, faithfulness, gentleness, and self-control."* How many sermons have we heard instructing us to produce these beautiful qualities? Whenever we tackle the task, we discover such ideals to be beyond our reach—that's because human striving has never, nor will it ever, produce something that can only be produced by the Spirit. It's not called the fruit of the Spirit for nothing!

If we are thoroughly convinced of our supernatural godlike status in terms of timeless eternity, nothing in the temporary realm has the power to intimidate us. No matter how big the problem, eternity always outranks time-encapsulated matters. *"I praise God for what He has promised. I trust in God, so why should I be afraid? What can mere mortals do to me?"* (Psalm 56:4)

In order to define our reborn-selves, we need to define God. In our limited knowledge of Him, we will never comprehend everything there is to know about Him, but whatever we learn of Him is a description of ourselves. In describing Him, we describe ourselves. We are so unified with Him that what is in Him is in us. The vine and the branches carry the same sap. *"Yes, I am the vine; you are the branches. Those who remain in Me, and I in them, will produce much fruit. For apart from Me you can do nothing"* (John 15:5).

Can you imagine how wonderful our relationships would be if we could have the gracious nature of God? Well the good news is that our nature is precisely the same as the divine nature of God. *"And because of His glory and excellence, He has given us great and precious promises. These are the promises that enable you to share His divine nature and escape the world's corruption caused by human desires"* (2Pet 1:4). This being the case, why aren't we experiencing the divine nature of God in practice? The answer is that by striving to obtain a divine nature, we are effectively denying that we already possess a divine nature!

Wouldn't it be wonderful to have the same glory that Jesus had? The good news is that we are just as glorious as Him. I can just see the religious squirm at the thought. "Blasphemy! Blasphemy!" It's painful to see sincere Christian's waiting in anticipation of the glory when they already share

Jesus' glory. He said, *"I have given them the glory You (the Father) gave Me..."* (John 17:22).

We often hear prayers like "Come Holy Spirit" as though He is out there somewhere. These prayers deny the reality of the ever present indwelling Holy Spirit. While we are looking elsewhere for the glory, we will not find it, because it is not out there, He resides within us!

Another misconception is that we are leaky vessels and are in constant need of Holy Spirit topping up. This thought denies the reality of what took place at rebirth. We and the Holy Spirit became one. For the Holy Spirit to leak out, our own spirit would have to leak out with Him. If we leaked out of our bodies, we would immediately expire.

Many may acknowledge the finished work of the cross, yet have difficulty accepting that it gave them a brand-new identity in God. In order for religion to survive, its followers must always be incomplete and require on-going spiritual adjustment—always looking for outside help—thus missing the obvious. All that God is, is already within them. They are like a policeman who is not prepared to make an arrest, because he is not convinced of his authority. Unless we grasp the gravity of what took place at rebirth, our authority is not going to scare Satan.

There are many takes on the river flowing from the temple, as described by Ezekiel. Often believers talk about being swept away by the Spirit as they are carried away by the river. Others have seen themselves as the trees along its banks, drawing nourishment from the river. Still others have seen themselves as the Dead Sea being refreshed by the Holy Spirit. All of these analogies cause us to see the flow as coming from an outside source.

While standing on the Mount of Olives, looking across the Kidron valley at the temple mount, I became aware that Ezekiel wasn't speaking metaphorically when he described the river flowing from beneath the temple, he was describing reality in advance. Water will literally pour out after an earthquake breaks an existing subterranean well. Apparently, geologists are aware of an enormous well beneath the temple mount, and a fault line that runs directly through it. End-time eschatology reveals that when Jesus' feet touch down on the Mount of Olives, there will be an almighty earthquake. This will literally release the motherlode of all gushers.

Sure, there are metaphorical parallels to be drawn from this seismic event. The most obvious should be that we, being the temple of the Holy Spirit, pour forth the water of the Holy Spirit from within us, refreshing stagnant waters and feeding trees which produce leaves and fruit for the benefit of all. But as long as we continue to expect a flow from an outside source, we will not acknowledge that there is a well within us; ready to overflow, feed, nourish and refresh.

"He that believeth on me, as the Scripture hath said, out of his belly shall flow rivers of living water" (John 7:38). It doesn't state that this only applies to those who are spiritually mature enough or holy enough. The only qualification stated is believing on Jesus—in other words, rebirth. For most believers, their wells are stopped up because they are on the lookout for another flow from somewhere else. For them, Sundays are no more than unfulfilled searches, as they leave yet another church meeting with unquenched thirsts. Our well cannot gush forth from within while we are looking for the stream to come to us from somewhere else. We need a fresh revelation of who we are in God. In discovering what He contains within himself, we discover what we contain within ourselves.

We and God are within one another. *"I am in them and You are in Me. May they experience such perfect unity that the world will know that You sent Me..."* (John 17:23). We don't live as isolated beings; we live in Him. We originate from God as His offspring. We are God's environment—His address on earth—it's where He lives. *"For in Him we live and move and exist. As some of your own poets have said, 'We are His offspring'"* (Act 17:28).

I am sure we all agree that Jesus is glorious. Well, if He is glorious then so are we. The very qualities we adore in Him, are duplicated in us (John 17:22).

Why is it that so many believers don't get to experience fullness of life? It is not that they don't love God enough. No, it is the other way around. They don't know how much they are loved! Here is the issue—we know ourselves only too well and can't see anything lovable about ourselves. I am sure we all agree that everything about Jesus is desirable. In as much as He is desirable to His Father, so are we! Unless we come to accept our similarity to Christ, our desirability will escape our notice. If we don't see ourselves as He sees us, we settle for living as though deficient and incomplete.

Unmerited favour is so easily forfeited. Our misplaced efforts at attempting to deserve God's attention, is the very thing that disqualifies us from receiving what He offers undeservedly. Our very efforts stand in the way. Besides, if we must do something, how can we possibly know whether we have done enough. If we are trying to be good enough for God's blessings, then it is obvious that we are not allowing ourselves the luxury of indulging in His goodness already deposited within us.

We need a revelation of how our Father relates to His beloved children. He loves them regardless—they are His nearest and dearest, and that's all that counts with Him. We are intensely loved, entirely complete and divinely powerful. *"May you experience the love of Christ, though it is too great to understand fully. Then you will be made complete with all the fullness of life and power that comes from God"* (Eph 3:19).

It is so easy to imagine God silently enjoying our worship of Him, but it is not something He does in silence. In the Song of Solomon, He demonstrates His love for us by responding to our loving advances with loving responses. As you whisper worshipful words in His ear, you may hear your Lover whispering sweet nothings back into your ear. As you tell

Him that He is glorious, He tells you that you are glorious—He made you glorious. As you tell Him of your love for Him, He tells you of His love for you. As you lift up His name, He lifts up your name. As you say, *"My lover is mine, and I am his..."* He says, *"Your love delights me, my treasure..."* (Song of Solomon 2:16, 4:10). He is smitten with you. Rather than live without you, He chose to die for you!

God is your Dad. Dads go to enormous lengths to support their children. Go to any school sporting event and watch parents misbehave as they lose their dignity, shouting advice to the referee, urging their children on. Although God doesn't misbehave, He nevertheless has the same fatherly heart, cheering us on, and then throwing His arms around us, no matter whether we win or lose. He is always for us; never against us!

We are complete in our union with Christ. When something is complete, it requires nothing more to be added. By adding our religious performance in an attempt to complete ourselves, we effectively deny our completion. We only benefit from this union to the extent that we acknowledge its completion. Denying it is as good as being incomplete. *"For in Christ lives all the fullness of God in a human body. So you also are complete through your union with Christ, who is the head over every ruler and authority"* (Col 2:9,10). We do not carry a fractional measure of God; we have the fullness of God. He could not possibly add an ounce more of Himself to us—we already have all of Him! With Him within, we have every bit as much of the miraculous power of God as Jesus had when He walked the Earth. In the same way that every spiritual ruler of darkness was subject to Him, every spiritual ruler of darkness is subject to us.

We often see sincere believers pleading for more of God. The sincerity of their hearts' cries come through loud and clear, but these prayers simply cannot be answered—all that God is, was given to them at rebirth. There is no more of Him to be had.

On the other hand, a prayer that God can answer is the one that Paul prayed in Ephesians 3:19 *"May you experience the love of Christ"*. You might be feeling that we ought to love God more. Undoubtedly yes! And that is why we need to have a revelation of His love for us. Without it, our love remains on a human level. On this level, love is seldom given without ulterior motives. Often love is given in order to get love, or at least to be thought well of by others and by God. No human has ever been fully capable of giving the pure unmerited agape love that God gives. When we are convinced that God loves us, despite our less than perfect living, the pressure is off—we cease to be so hard on ourselves. His love for us gives us permission to love ourselves. And loving Him comes naturally—we love Him because He first loved us.

The love that we receive from Him gives us something of value to spread around. It enables us to love others somewhat more in the way that He loves us. It all starts with understanding that we are loved regardless of our imperfections. The more we discover of His love for us, the more we discover ourselves loving others and can give no explanation for it! Because we get it undeservedly, we find ourselves giving it away undeservedly. Without the influence of His agape kind of love, our love remains tainted with self-interest.

Tragically, many sincere believers have been told that there is more of God to be had. Who can blame them for being disenchanted? They are exhausted and tired of chasing. God loves us as passionately as He loves Jesus. Jesus said to the Father, *"You love them as much as You love Me"* (John 17:23). Before we did anything worthy of love, we were already the focus of God's love. Then when we fell into deep sin, His love towards us never even skipped a beat.

It is not unusual for believers to misconstrue this scripture, believing it to be a command to do something to obtain His love. But it is not a command; it is a declaration of His love for us. He doesn't expect us to prove ourselves. In trying to impress God with our holiness, we effectively deny that we are already fully accepted in Christ. Sadly, we are so easily side-tracked into Christian performance, thereby forfeiting our covenant privileges. If we are chasing after something we already have, we are chasing the wind. So many spend a lifetime doing it. Religion can be oh so empty!

Satan is happy to see God's people chasing after stuff they already have—happy to see religion disinheriting them! If he can keep us busy enough chasing our tails, we won't discover who we actually are, and consequently won't pose a threat to his diabolical mischief. Religion is as harmful to believers as wilful sin. Religion runs on the high-octane fuel of "Christian" performance—keeping sincere believers "busy for God". Like a hamster, always busy on his wheel, they get nowhere fast. The relationship they so desperately desire and strive for, is unknowingly already theirs. What a crying shame to miss it with such sincerity!

Now don't get me wrong. Good works are commendable—they just don't get us more of God.

Denying that we are like Him leaves us functioning no better than we did when we were unsaved. If we see ourselves as anything other than godlike, we will live lives that are less than godlike, and if we live less than godlike:

- We can't live like Jesus.
- We'll be spiritually hamstrung.
- We'll have difficulty accepting that we are unconditionally loved.
- Our authority will not carry godly clout.
- Our good prayers will lack confidence.
- Our good witnessing will lack conviction.
- Our good leadership will lack God's inspiration.
- Our good preaching will not be life changing.
- Our good business skills will lack God's favour (unfair advantage).

- Our good parenting will lack divine wisdom.
- Our good relationships will lack depth.
- Our praise and worship will be shallow.
- We'll do our best to change ourselves, but with little success.
- Our holy making attempts will disappoint.
- We won't have a princely perspective of our reign over life.
- Intimacy with our Father on this level will be limited.

"For we died and were buried with Christ by baptism. And just as Christ was raised from the dead by the glorious power of the Father, now we also may live new lives" (Rom 6:4).

When Jesus died, we died. The person we once were, no longer exists. This scripture is not calling on us to die to our old lives. We already died—we had to die in order to be re-born. Our baptism confirmed it. It is not a future ongoing process—death is profoundly final. The old you, that sinful old man no longer exists.

"Not so Deon", you might be thinking, "The Bible requires me to die daily to the things of this world". Sure, you should, but be careful to know what you are dying to. You are to die to your old habits and corrupt thinking, but you are not to die to your old man of sin. That man did not survive your death and rebirth.

If we get this wrong, we end up shadow boxing an imaginary enemy, and Satan steps aside to watch with glee as we beat ourselves to a pulp. He gets a freebee as we do his dirty work for him free of charge. He knows our self-esteem will take a beating, our confidence will wane, and our faith will falter.

As much as we would rather not, we all know that we continue to sin, but thankfully, our sinning does not take place in our rebirthed sinless spirits—they are sealed in perpetual righteousness (Eph 1:13). Sin can only take place in our minds (the soulish part of ourselves). But Satan has a hard time tempting a mind led by the Spirit.

Can our spirits be corrupted? Most certainly not—we were born of incorruptible seed (I Peter 1:23).

The old man that we once were was crucified with Christ, never to be resurrected again. Our new man came about when God Himself came to live within our bodies, making the two of us one single new person. *"But he that is joined unto the Lord is one spirit"* (1 Co 6:17 KJV). There are not two spirits knocking around within us—there is only one—the one that was born of God's Spirit! When our spirits were fused together with God's, we were transformed into the god-class of being!

If we conduct our lives well, living by impeccable principles, with wisdom in every decision, yet fail to recognise that we are in the same class of being as our heavenly Dad, we will never know the God empowerment lying latent within us. If we are not entirely convinced of our kingly status, we will suffer unnecessarily. Unless we exercise the authority we have, Satan will have a field day wreaking havoc and mayhem!

"As He is, so are we in this world" (1 John 4:17 KJV).

It is important to grasp the gravity of our similarity to Jesus. For far too long, Christians have belittled themselves in the name of piety, thinking this would impress God. We are sons and daughters of God. A son is of the same species as his father. Dogs can't father cats and cats can't father rats. We take after our earthly parents in so many ways, and it is no different with our heavenly Father—very much alike in Spirit!

Why is it important to know how similar we are to our Heavenly Father? If we want to operate in godly authority, we must know who it is that is behind our authority—it is our Dad! He is a dad like no other! When He speaks to us, we know that we have been spoken to! When we speak in His name, Satan knows he has been spoken to! As a small child, I can remember settling arguments with my little brother and sister. When they wouldn't take my word for it, they would demand, "Who said?" I would answer, "Daddy said!" And that would settle the argument!

Obviously, children are of the same species as their fathers. Let's face it, we don't have a closer relative than the Father who gave us second birth—and that makes us one and the same species—we are the spitting image of God our Father! Just as God is the Creator, so are we creators, with a small "c" of course. Just as God created everything with His words, He has instructed us to create with our words. Just as demons must bow their knees to Jesus, they must bow their knees to us when we command them in His name.

Isn't it heresy to regard ourselves to be like God? It's not heresy if He chose to make us in His likeness. If His word says, *"As He is so are we in this world,"* and we choose to disagree, surely that is what heresy is! In making ourselves out to be less than the god-class for the sake of appearing to be humble, is not what humility is; it is what pride is! It takes pride to disagree with God. After all, isn't it His idea that we are family?

We are not gods because we say we are, we are gods because Jesus says we are. Jesus answered them, *"Is it not written in your law, I said, Ye are gods?"* (John 10:34 KJV).

God sent His son to the cross so that He would become the firstborn of many brethren. Did you notice that our relationship with Jesus is not that of servants but siblings? We have the same relationship with the Father as He has. Our Father doesn't have any favourites, not even Jesus is more of a favourite with heavenly Father than us. When Jesus prayed to the Father, He stated that the Father loves you and me as much as He loves Jesus. He could not have made it any plainer; He has no favourites!

Doesn't this just make you want to leap up and dance for joy? Do you see yourself as a kid at home with Papa, enjoying the self-same privileges He bestows upon His beloved Son, Jesus?

Strangers don't just come off the street and take what they want from your pantry, do they? But your children are at liberty to do so. A duplicate of every treasure chest in heaven exists within every born-again believer. These treasure chests, like bank vaults, have two keys; the one is our identity, and the other, the name of Jesus. Both keys are required to be turned simultaneously.

Well let's see how similar we are to our Father: We operate in His faith. We speak His creative words. We love with the love of the Lord. We share a common enemy. We come against our common enemy with decisive authority, in precisely the same way Jesus did.

If we are so much alike, in what way is He superior to us? He is:

- all powerful (omnipotent)
- all knowing (omniscient)
- present everywhere at the same time (omnipresent)
- owner of the universe
- outside of time and space
- accountable to nobody

Though we are of the god species, we are like Him yet less than Him:

- we are not all powerful
- we do not know everything
- we can only be in one place at a time
- we have not been granted dominion beyond the earth
- we are restricted to time and space
- we are accountable to God

God wanted intimacy with us. Just as you cannot have true intimacy with your budgie, so He could not be intimate with a lesser species than Himself. He desires the fellowship of beings who are similar to Himself. To make this possible, He had to birth Himself into us, thus transforming us into His class of being.

Instead of wiping us off the face of the Planet, as we so rightly deserved, He chose a better route—rebirthing us into righteousness—choosing to share His Spirit with new-born sinless creatures. In so doing, intimacy with mankind would be a real possibility—opening the way for His original plan for humanity.

At creation, what did God breath into Adam to give him life? Was it oxygen? No! God doesn't need oxygen to stay alive; it was He Himself that He breathed into Adam, making him a godlike-being within an earthly body. Unfortunately, Adam sold mankind's godlike status to Satan! As an opportunist of note, he grabbed it with both hands, perverting it for his own evil purposes. But thankfully, Jesus, the Son of God, stepped in to correct Adam's catastrophic blunder, restoring believer's status back to that of sons of God!

Jesus didn't come to crush us into submission. No! He came to elevate us! Not to snuff out smouldering flaxes, but to breathe life into smouldering flaxes! He wants us to discover how limitless our godly standing is; not to discover how weak and ineffective we are. After all, it was His idea to elevate us to godlikeness! Sadly, many are saved only to have their hopes dashed. Why were we saved in the first place? Was it not to fulfil our hopes? How sad it is that so many of us never come to discover our exalted position as kings and priests!

Our Father is the King of kings. Who are the kings that He is King over? Are they the ruling monarchs of states? Surely, the Hitlers of this world are not taking their instructions from the King of kings. Who then are the kings that God is King over? Kings' children are kings and princes in their own rights. When He says that He is the King of kings, He means that He is the King of His own royal descendants, all who are born of His seed!

As for the tyrannical kings of this world, we know that every knee will bow and every tongue will confess that Jesus Christ is Lord in the sweet by and by, but right here and now, these evil kings are certainly not acting as though they are under the lordship of the King of kings. Yes, He appoints and dismisses kings, but that does not mean that they are submitted to His Lordship. Surely, the Kingdom of God only exists on Earth where He is invited to reign. Is that not what we, His children have been authorised to do? We have the distinct honour of being kings submitted to the lordship of the King of kings.

If you are still not entirely convinced that ordinary believers have godly status, then perhaps we should let scripture have the final say. What does the Bible have to say about the status of God's children?

The Psalmist said *"I say, 'You are gods; you are all children of the Most High'"* (Psalm 82:6). Then Jesus said *"I say, you are gods!"* (John 10:34).

Don't confuse this truth with the New Age Movement which teaches that we don't need rebirth because we are already our own gods. What a distortion—I hope you recognise who the author of this subtle twist to God's truth is. The Mormons have their own bent on this issue. These ideas fail the test of authenticity—they do not offer a solution to the fiery destiny of un-regenerated humanity. They believe that they are accountable to themselves, but in reality, we are accountable to God. They are burdened with the task of cleansing themselves; whereas we are released from such onerousness, being cleansed by the blood of Jesus. They depend on their goodness, while we depend on God's goodness.

I must be honest, when I first discovered my imputed godly status, my treasured theology was seriously upset. It forced me to give it serious consideration, checking it out in scripture. I must admit that I did so with scepticism. Had I come upon a trick of the enemy to draw me away from God? To my surprise, the better I understood my similarity to God, the closer I was drawn to Him. This truth makes a Father/son relationship ever much more intimate.

The early translators of the Bible had the same problem with this concept. In fact, they had such difficulty getting their minds around what the original Hebrew text had to say about our godly status, that they purposely chose to mistranslate scripture. They just could not get their minds around the reality of their godlikeness. *"For thou hast made him a little lower than the angels, and hast crowned him with glory and honor"* (Psa 8:5 KJV). This is not what the original Hebrew text says, and therefore this translation is plain and simply heresy. We were not made a little lower than the angels, we were made a little lower than "Elohim". Elohim is one of God's names. Subsequent translators have come to terms with this stupendous error. The New Living Translation correctly reads *"Yet You made them only a little lower than God and crowned them with glory and honor"* (Psalm 8:5). The truth is, we are not lower than the angels, we are not even a whole lot lower than God. This scripture correctly identifies us as just a *"little"* bit lower than God. In the same way that our children are not lower than us in so far as human genetics are concerned; they certainly are lower than us in so far as maturity is concerned. That's how it is with our heavenly Father and His children.

Like the early translators, you may be having difficulty fitting this idea into your theology. Don't make the same mistake—don't deny your God-established position. If you do, this is not all you will lose. You will forfeit your right to reign in life as God does. *"For if by one man's offense death reigned by one; much more they which receive abundance of grace and of the gift of righteousness shall reign in life by one, Jesus Christ"* (Rom 5:17).

Some may not be bold enough to reign in life—boldness may come across as arrogance to religious thinkers. They may have become accustomed to taking life's knocks as though they deserve nothing better.

Then, when it comes to holiness, they may have been lulled into contentment; satisfied with their attempts at restraining themselves. But unless iniquities have been conquered at heart level, they have not been conquered at all—likely to rear their ugly heads in unguarded moments.

Religion is all about self-effacing; while grace is all about empowering! Our sonship empowers us to rise and shine as conquerors, victors and overcomers. But we cannot do so unless we know that we are preordained to be sons of God. It is all about acknowledging the status endowed upon us at rebirth and walking in the authority of it.

As already mentioned, Jesus didn't come to make us better people; He came to make us sons, the same species as Himself. Each and every one of His children have heavenly citizenship—diplomatic passports with earthly visas. We are no longer citizens of this Earth; we are heavenly citizens seconded to the Earth as emissaries for the purpose of exercising divinely ordained decisive dominion. We are to bring every earthly challenge into subjection to divine rulership. As much as our Father wishes to rule on Earth, He only rules where His children rule. They are divine conduits of His love and rulership.

If both the psalmist and Jesus said that we are gods, then who are we to reject such a truth? Let's face it, it is not at all smart to disagree with God! Seeing He is in the god-class, how can His children be of a different species? Deny this truth if you will, but do so with the understanding that your denial will cost you your God ordained spiritual effectiveness. In acknowledging our Godlikeness, all kinds of supernatural possibilities arise!

We were not born again to live human lives limited to our humanity. At rebirth we became a new species that never existed before; a godlike species living in human bodies. We and the Holy Spirit became one new complex being, "Children of the living God". We take after our heavenly Daddy, just as our earthly children take after us.

If my daughters don't look a bit like me, then I must ask some very serious questions. If they look more like the postman, then something is mighty suspicious! Thankfully, it is obvious that my eldest daughter is mine. We both have the same gangly stride when we jog—unmistakably a Stevens. By the same token, we are definitely our heavenly Father's children, taking after Him in so many ways!

We are not supposed to be humans trying to achieve what can only be achieved by gods. Obviously, as God's sons, the word "impossible" ceases to have a place in our vocabulary—everything is possible!

Isn't it interesting that Jesus did not only commission us to do the works that He did; He commissioned us to do even greater works than He did? I think it is safe to say that the vast majority of believers do not perform greater miracles than Jesus. Most believers could not even imagine themselves doing the miracles Jesus did. But when we understand our godly status, godly possibilities arise! We share His DNA, His infinite power and His priceless wisdom.

If it were not for God's children ruling on this earth, God would have no legal authority to reign over it. Though His Holy Ghost is ever present here, He still needs the credentials of mere mortals' dominion to carry out His plans. We should not be taken aback by this information, afterall, it is His idea to rule and reign by invitation. As almighty as He is, He still looks to His children to carry out His purposes.

"Heal the sick, raise the dead, cure those with leprosy, and cast out demons. Give as freely as you have received!" (Mat 10:8).

In this scripture, Jesus didn't say that we should ask the Father to heal the sick, as though He must do miracles for us; He said that "we" are to heal the sick. Sounds like He wants "us" to step out and do the healing ourselves, doesn't it? And that being the case, there is more to us than meets the eye. As sons, we are to rule and govern, not as humans, but as divinely empowered sons of God.

So often we hear prayers offered from a position of weakness. I've often prayed that way myself. To be honest, we don't always feel strong. But contrary to our feeble feelings, we are always strong in the Spirit. Our power is not measured in feelings—it is measured by what the word of God has to say about our rebirth.

"All praise to God, the Father of our Lord Jesus Christ, who has blessed us with every spiritual blessing in the heavenly realms because we are united with Christ" (Eph 1:3).

We are not strong because we feel that way, we are strong because we are united with Christ. When we feel low, we need to remind ourselves of our unity with divinity.

Isn't it interesting that this scripture says that we already have *"every"* possible spiritual blessing? No matter how hard we may pray, God simply cannot add another blessing to *"every"* blessing—something with which we have already been endowed. It happened at the precise moment of our rebirth. Once endowed with the indwelling Holy Spirit, what more can possibly be added? All that God is, is contained within the Holy Spirit now dwelling within us!

If you are feeling low because you've failed God in some way, this passage of scripture goes on to say, *"Even before He made the world, God loved us and chose us in Christ to be holy and without fault in His eyes"* (Eph 1:4). Take heart! You are not unworthy; in God's sight you are holy and without a single fault! This verse is not a command for you to be holy and faultless; it declares that you are holy and faultless in His eyes.

"Doesn't this just let us off the hook at a time when we really should feel guilty?"

"Yes!" That's what the good news is all about! Let's make up our minds: Are we holy and faultless because of our behaviour, or because of what Jesus did for us?

"If that is so, then I am just going to go out there and have a good time sinning myself silly. Is that okay then?"

Seriously? Let's get real: *"Since we have died to sin, how can we continue to live in it?"* (Rom 6:2).

Does this prayer sound familiar to you? "Jesus, I am weak and you are strong. Please heal me." I have heard it more times than I would like to admit—I have been guilty of praying it myself. There are three main problems with this prayer:

1.   It denies the power residing within us. *"I also pray that you will understand the incredible greatness of God's power for us who believe Him. This is the same mighty power that raised Christ from the dead and seated Him in the place of honor at God's right hand in the heavenly realms"* (Eph 1:19,20). You might be thinking, "What about John 15:5 which states that apart from Me you can do nothing?" This is true, but don't lose sight of the fact that we are never apart from Him! Hebrews 13:5 makes it perfectly clear that He will never leave us nor forsake us. We need never pray from a point of weakness—all the power we will ever need already resides within us.

2.   It asks God to do something that He has already done. 1 Peter 2:24 says that by His stripes we were healed—past tense. To answer the above prayer, Jesus would have to be whipped all over again. No! That's not necessary; our healing was fully accomplished two thousand years ago—it's a done deal!

3.   It pleads for healing to come to us from above. That's not where healing comes from. All healing power already resides within us. We are to *"give (healing) as freely as (we) have received (healing)!"* (Mat 10:8). In the prayer of healing, we are not to obtain healing, we are to give healing just as freely as we received the power to heal. We obtained it in one and the same package at rebirth. Peter prayed a model prayer when he told the lame beggar, "Such as I have give I thee: In the name of Jesus Christ of Nazareth rise up and walk" (Acts 3:6 KJV). This prayer produced a remarkable healing. We all received the exact same Spirit as Peter at rebirth. That being the case, why did He experience more remarkable miracles than us? Electricity is in our homes even when we are not using it. We only benefit from it when we flick the switch. Although we have the same power Peter had, we haven't flicked the switch. We thought that if we prayed long and hard enough, God would flick His switch. Big mistake! Sadly, this misunderstanding led us to conclude that it wasn't God's will to heal us, so we just gave up believing and allowed sickness to reign.

How do we flick the switch? It's not about speaking to God; it's about speaking to the mountain. Jesus promised that we would have everything that we say. *"Whosoever shall say unto this mountain, Be thou removed, and be thou cast into the sea; and shall not doubt in his heart, but shall believe that those things which he saith shall come to pass; he shall have whatsoever he saith"* (Mar 11:23 KJV).

Does speaking to things sound a bit quirky? Jesus didn't think so—He spoke to a fig tree, sicknesses, handicaps and demons. You may be thinking that it was different for Jesus. Why would you think that? The same Spirit that was in Jesus is in us. The apostles had no problem with this; it's the very same way that they dealt with sicknesses.

Healing does not come from above; it comes from within—that's where God put it. Praying to God for healing is a prayer that God simply cannot answer. In view of the fact that there is not a single instance recorded in the New Testament of the apostles ever asking God to heal, but umpteen recordings of them commanding sickness to go, or for healing to come, where did we ever get the idea that we should ask God for healing? Yet it is by far the most common way that believers pray for healing.

Just as the judgement for our sin fell on Jesus, two thousand years ago, so did our sicknesses. He has done everything necessary for all to be healed—now it is up to us to appropriate what He achieved.

If we were sitting on a well in the desert and didn't know it, we could die of thirst. We all have a well full of divine healing within us. If we are not aware of it, we may be enduring sickness unnecessarily. Praise God, we can send the bucket down within us to draw out as much as we need for ourselves, and for anybody else who may need it.

Believe me, if we don't reign in life, somebody else will! Better that it be us! We may not always reign well, but at least we'll be better off than being reigned over by one who kills, steals and destroys!

"And I will give you the keys of the Kingdom of Heaven. Whatever you forbid on earth will be forbidden in heaven, and whatever you permit on earth will be permitted in heaven" (Mat 16:19).

Can you get your mind around such enormous authority? It's not what God binds and permits, it's what we bind and permit that stymies the enemy. All well and good, but what happens when we fail to bind and permit? Sadly, our negligence allows Satan far too much leeway to carry out his dastard plans against us. Satan only has as much power and authority as we allow him. Failure to reign is as good as asking a burglar to house-sit your home, or a paedophile to babysit your children.

My daughter, Carmen, phoned me in a hysterical panic. Her ex-husband had been fighting for custody of their infant son. He threatened to do whatever it would take to achieve his goal. As a strong character, he was accustomed to getting his way. He felt he could make a case for gaining custody because her employment required her to travel extensively.

I immediately took authority over the spirit that was behind this attack and asked for a wonderful blessing to overwhelm the man. The next morning, I got a phone call from Carmen. She had heard from her ex and was amazed at the change that had come over him. No longer belligerent and manipulative, but apologetic, caring and concerned, dropping his claim for custody. Since then, he has proved to be a wonderful caring father, maintaining a healthy relationship with Carmen and our family.

Taking authority over the spirit instead of the man, had achieved the impossible, and saved Carmen a long and costly legal wrangle.

When the storm came up and tossed the disciples' boat about, they woke Jesus in a panic. How did Jesus restore order? How did He subdue the waves? Interestingly, He said nothing to the waves, but chose rather to command the wind to subside. No wind equalled no waves. We are so apt to fight the waves in our lives and in the lives of others, instead of dealing with the wind responsible for the waves. Visible behaviour is not the problem; it is the invisible spirit behind the behaviour that is the problem.

When taking authority, it is important to attack the spirit behind the behaviour and not the misbehaving person. We are to bless the person, no matter how contrary he or she may seem to be. Attacking the person is diabolical to marriages, friendships, families, businesses and churches.

We might as well get used to it—church people are always going to disappoint each other! The act of taking offence is the number one cause of schisms and church splits. It is not the offender; it is the offence taker that brings a church to ruin. Offence taking is the most blatant evidence of gracelessness! Satan's strategy is to divide and conquer. For as long as he can get us to go for the person rather than for the spirit behind the behaviour, he can wreck any church and relationship at will. We should recognise his tactics and not take the bait. Attacking a friend always results in personal loss—equivalent to self-mutilation!

Some derogatory rumours concerning my business were doing the rounds. A meeting was called, so that my accusers could air their grievances. The accusations were serious enough to put me out of business. Before going into the meeting, I took authority over the spirits that were responsible for the rumours and prayed a rich blessing over my accusers. I made up my mind not to be defensive, but rather to leave my defence in the hands of the Holy Spirit.

The chairman of the meeting opened the floor for the accusers to state their cases. To his surprise, not one of them spoke up. The silence was thick—you could cut it with a knife. After a while, the chairman became impatient and threatened to close the meeting unless someone spoke up. Still no accusations! Finally, one spoke up saying, "I respect Deon and have absolutely no problem with him, but I have heard a rumour." Instead of accusing me, they all decided to pledge their support for my business as never before.

God had granted me decisive victory! Something for which I could not take credit—I didn't even open my mouth. But then again, I had not dealt with the waves; I had dealt with the wind behind the waves. With Satan taken out of the equation, their huge balloon of accusations just hung limply. What the enemy had intended for my harm, God had miraculously turned to my benefit.

When taking authority over a spirit, it is vitally important to let the offending party off the hook. We are to give him or her a gift they do not deserve. Afford them the same grace that we desire from God for ourselves. Considering the abundance of grace God extends to us as offenders, how is it even remotely possible of us to fail to extend similar grace to those who offend us?

I had mentioned this predicament to my pastor while in the sauna at our local gym. He immediately took authority over the spirit of revenge.

About six months later, while this matter was still weighing heavily on my mind, the CEO of our company wrote to me. Instead of reprimanding me, he invited Susan and me to attend an awards function at a topflight venue in Johannesburg. All our board members, our shareholders and our top clients—the captains of South African industry, were flown in for the auspicious black-tie event. Before this distinguished audience, awards were conferred for innovation, initiative and integrity. Out of a staff of thousands, only one was honoured for integrity. Guess who got the award? The very thing that Satan had attacked, God had favoured. It should not have come as a surprise. After all, my pastor and I had dealt with the wind behind the waves, and God had turned what was meant for my harm into a great personal advantage.

In the long history of our Company, integrity had never before been awarded in this way. It wasn't any of the thousands of deserving staff members who received the award; it came to the one who dared to take the devil on, while forgiving his accusers. Praise God! He had moved a mighty corporation to bless a devil beater!

Although God's sons are enabled to walk in decisive authority, most of them will never do so. If we are under the impression that we need to pray, and then wait and see if God answers, we are obviously not walking in our authority. Good men do not have to do something bad to make things go wrong; things go wrong when good men do nothing. When we are not using our authority, Satan is quick to take the gap!

"A woman in the crowd had suffered for twelve years with constant bleeding, [having spent everything she had on doctors] and she could find no cure. Coming up behind Jesus, she touched the fringe of His robe. Immediately, the bleeding stopped. 'Who touched Me?' Jesus asked. Everyone denied it, and Peter said, 'Master, this whole crowd is pressing

up against You.' But Jesus said, 'Someone deliberately touched Me, for I felt healing power go out from Me.' When the woman realized that she could not stay hidden, she began to tremble and fell to her knees in front of Him. The whole crowd heard her explain why she had touched Him and that she had been immediately healed. 'Daughter,' He said to her, 'your faith has made you well. Go in peace'" (Luke 8:43-48).

This account makes it crystal clear that this woman was healed, not because Jesus decided to heal her, but because she decided she would be healed. Jesus didn't even know who was healed—He just felt healing power leave Him. We are not supposed to wonder whether our prayers will be answered; we are supposed to decide for ourselves. Did you get that? God doesn't decide on the outcome of our prayers for healing; we decide on the outcome. Jesus explained whose faith it was that had made her well—He said, "YOUR FAITH has made you well."

"I tell you, you can pray for anything, and if you believe that you've received it, it will be yours" (Mar 11:24). It's not about God's decision; it's about our decision. When Jesus said, *"Pray for anything,"* He really meant what He said—decide on whatever you desire, believe it is yours and it is yours.

Anything? Seriously Jesus? That's pretty wide, isn't it? Surely such an all-encompassing invitation is open to abuse? Doesn't it play directly into the hands of greedy people? A valid question. But in practice, those who abuse it never get very far; they ask amiss (Jas 4:3). To walk at this level of emphatic faith, requires one to be attuned to both the word of God and the heart of God—our desires to be fashioned by His desires.

Are there some issues that are outside of our authority? Yes, as in Mark 10:35-40, where James and John asked to be seated on the right and left side of Jesus' throne in heaven. This was outside of their earthly domain. We don't have dominion over heaven. It is important to know what we have dominion over. Unless we know this, how could we possibly reign decisively? Clearly, sickness, lack, burdens and broken relationships are some of the issues we are to reign over.

"And hath put all things under his feet, and gave him to be the head over all things to the church, Which is his body, the fulness of him that filleth all in all" (Eph 1:22-23KJV).

If everything is under His feet, then we, being His body, have everything under our feet. When we are confronted with a burden, we should not look up as though it is towering over us, we should look down, because that is where we will find it—beneath our feet. Now it is up to us to subdue it!

"But the person who is joined to the Lord is one spirit with Him" (I Cor 6:17). God is not out there, many galaxies away. He is not even a separate being living within us. Though we are containers of God, we are complex beings—godlike beings. If religion has told us otherwise, then maybe we should change our perspectives. God is not only for us, He lives within us as part and parcel of who we are. Just as fruit cordial mixes with water when poured into a drinking glass to become a cocktail, so it is with our godlike status. When the Holy Spirit integrated Himself with us, we became entirely different entities. The Bible refers to us as, *"new creatures in Christ Jesus."* The same Spirit that raised Jesus from the dead, does not merely dwell within us; He has combined Himself with us.

As a man thinks in his heart so is he. If you think you are not what God said you are, you cannot be what He said you can be, nor have what He said you can have. Isn't it sobering to imagine that our opinion of ourselves plays such a crucial role in life? It either gives us access to Kingdom privileges or disqualifies us from them. Our thoughts are pivotal—establishing either victory or defeat in our daily encounters. If our thinking is so crucial, then we need to get to know what God has to say about who we are.

According to Him, we are His sons—the apple does not fall far from the tree. We are so much alike, for as He is so are we! Is He righteous? Yes! So are we (we are the righteousness of God in Christ). Is He a conqueror? Yes! So are we (in fact we are more than conquerors). Is He an overcomer? Yes! So are we (we overcome with the blood of the lamb and with the word of our testimony). Is He a victor? Yes! So are we (we are led in triumphant procession with Christ Jesus). Is He a Creator? Yes! So are we (with a small c of course). Is He complete? Yes! So are we (complete in our spirit man). Is He a king? Yes! So are we (yet accountable to the King of kings). Is He like His Father? Yes! So are we!

Seeing that we are intrinsically different to our former un-regenerated selves, we need to invest time to discover what we have become, and then convince ourselves of our godlike status. Decisive rulership cannot be exercised from a position of weakness—we need to be thoroughly convinced of our authority in order to live from a position of invincible strength. When we have God's perspective, the miraculous becomes normal.

"Henceforth I call you not servants" (John 15:15 KJV). We are not slaves, we are not even servants; we are sons, heirs and joint-heirs together with Christ. As joint-heirs, whatever Jesus owns, we own! All the wealth of heaven has been bequeathed jointly to us and Jesus. We don't get it when we get to heaven; it's already ours!

It's important to understand that we are not given this imperial status for the purpose of ruling over each other. That would be devilish! We are to rule over the responsibilities that God has given to each of us. This would include ruling over sickness, lack, habits, failure, discouragement and defeat in our careers, homes, relationships, investments, incomes etc.

We are not to strive to be sons—such striving would only serve to disinherit us! Sadly, so many relegate inheritance to a future date. Once we are convinced that we really are in the God-class of being, we can translate this knowledge into decisive rulership. Religion is about striving, but why would we strive for something that we already own? Tragically many do!

We don't have the Kingdom of God within us to make us feel good, although nobody could blame us for feeling good; we have the kingdom of God within us to wield decisive authority in exactly the same way Jesus did. He didn't just come to Earth to live and die for us; He came to demonstrate how to live victoriously. Our living should emulate His living—not one iota less miraculous.

The power we possess exceeds the power of any earthly superpower. The USSR of the past, and the mighty USA of the present, are no match for the power that exists within the least likely of us. How sad to believe, as many do, that we are victims of circumstances.

Jesus is the firstborn among many brethren. Brothers carry traces of their parents' DNA. They are alike in so many ways—both Jesus and we have the same Father—we resemble Him—A chip off the old block!

"Listen to Me, all who hope for deliverance—all who seek the LORD! Consider the rock from which you were cut, the quarry from which you were mined" (Isa 51:1). A geologist doesn't have to see the whole rock to determine its value, he only needs to inspect a tiny chip—he knows that the chip contains identical metals and minerals to the rock from which it was hewn. We are a chip hewn from the "Rock of Ages". The very elements within Him are within us.

I have always been told to look to Jesus, and then try to be like Him, but scripture tells a different story. It instructs us to look for God's image in our reborn selves. After all, we are the split image of our Dad. There is no need to try to be like Jesus. In doing so, we are pretending, faking another person's identity. The church has enough flakes—no need to add ourselves to the number.

"Flaky church people? You're kidding me!" In truth, the more demand placed on us to be like somebody else, albeit Jesus, the flakier we get.

The good news is that Christ, in the person of the Holy Spirit, has become one with our spirits. Who better to behave like Jesus than Jesus himself? After all, He behaves like Himself all the time, doesn't He?

Life is so much simpler when we allow Christ to live His life His way through us. Without effort, our behaviour becomes godly behaviour. How do we achieve this? Certainly not by striving. Only by allowing our god-like spirits to dictate how we act and re-act, do we have victory over our actions. Sadly, we often allow circumstances to lead us by our noses.

"I will proclaim the name of the LORD; how glorious is our God! He is the Rock; His deeds are perfect. Everything He does is just and fair. He is a faithful God who does no wrong; how just and upright He is! ... You neglected the Rock who had fathered you; you forgot the God who had given you birth" (Deut 32:3,4 & 18).

Unsaved people are the geologists, inspecting our Father's character as displayed in the behaviour of His children. When we yield to Christ within, His glory manifests outwardly—it is something that simply cannot be forced—it is the fruit of the Spirit! While His fruit is manifesting in our actions, we can relax—our weaknesses and unhealthy habits need no further modification. Before we know it, to our surprise and delight, we discover that we are no longer a slave to unhealth behaviour! Once we have put the Spirit in control, there is no further need to subdue our anger, self-centeredness, jealousy and greed—Christ's behaviour is always Christ-like! No need to watch our every word—the pressure is off—life is a breeze!

God doesn't have worms for sons, yet tragically, many sincere believers think God would be impressed with them for regarding themselves as worms. But He does not respond to humble worms—He responds to audaciously bold Christlike sons and daughters—their audacity tempered only by their submission to His will.

New Creatures

When Jesus was crucified, we were crucified. When Jesus died, we died. When Jesus was buried, we were buried. You cannot be deader than dead and buried! When Jesus was quickened, we were quickened. When Jesus was raised from the dead, we were raised from the dead as brand new creations without a past. Our prior lives, whether exemplary or errant, are simply not on record in heaven.

"For you were buried with Christ when you were baptized. And with Him you were raised to new life because you trusted the mighty power of God, who raised Christ from the dead" (Col 2:12).

Our past is dead and buried. The person we were is still in the casket. When we were acquitted, the docket containing the charges against us was destroyed, and every accusation permanently expunged from heaven's record books.

We do not have to strive to become sinless new creatures. Sinlessness is not something that can be achieved—it can only be conferred by rebirth. The new creature that rose to life has no past and is entirely incapable of being contaminated by future sin. *"To wit, that God was in Christ, reconciling the world unto himself, not imputing their trespasses unto them; and hath committed unto us the word of reconciliation"* (2Co 5:19 KJV). Isn't this just the best news ever? God is not imputing your sins to you; He is imputing them to Jesus!

Some Christians spend a lifetime striving to be like Jesus. I John 4:17 (KJV) says, *"As he is, so are we in this world."* Did you notice, we are not going through a process of improving ourselves to eventually become like Him? We were raised back to life to be the spitting image of Him—it happened in a nanosecond at rebirth.

Many strive to raise themselves to life. It's painful to watch them destroying their joy with false humility and meaningless religiosity. Frankly, they are wasting valuable time and energy—no matter how hard they may try, resurrection cannot be repeated. Relax, the work of resurrection is a fate accompli!

The fact that they are not experiencing new life does not prove that they do not have new life; it simply proves that they don't understand what they have. It's not a matter of not being one with God; it's a matter of not grasping the potential established by our oneness with Him. His empowerment is all encompassing—impacting everything concerning us! It affects the way we behave, the things we desire, our every hope, aspiration and so much more! We cannot use what we have been equipped with, unless of course, we get to know what we have been equipped with. You could live the life of a pauper, even if you had a winning lotto ticket in your bottom draw and didn't know it.

You died a sinner—that person no longer exists. You were raised up as the righteousness of God—a completely different species of being—a godlike human, a son who takes after his Father, carrying His Spirit, His divine nature and His DNA.

We are not just sinners saved by grace. In this statement the tense is wrong. It would be more correct to say that we "were" sinners saved by grace. We lost our sinner identity at rebirth. That person no longer exists—he or she was terminated before a new sinless person could be rebirthed. Righteousness cannot be conferred upon sinners—it can only be conferred upon new creatures. Our new identities are spotless—never to be tarnished—not by sinful pasts, sinful presents or sinful futures!

"This sounds all well and good," you might be saying, "But unfortunately, the reality is that I continue to sin despite my rebirth. Doesn't this make nonsense of this notion?" No! Not at all! All that it proves is that while your spirit is not capable of sinning, because it is a new creation born of incorruptible seed, your soul remains susceptible to sin, and will need more than a lifetime to bring it into alignment with your sinless spirit. Change takes place little by little as we devote time to renewing our minds to this truth. It is not a once off happening; it's a lifestyle! It is only when we come to accept that we are every bit like Christ, that unforced Christ-like actions follow. When we stop striving and allow ourselves to be Spirit led, we get real!

If we would allow our spirits to be in charge of our every thought, there would be no further need to guard our every word and action. Sin is only possible when our five senses are in charge. While we are controlled by our spirits, our bodies will be protesting—demanding the opposite. Although our spirits contain the power to heal us, our bodies are going to scream out for attention, telling us that we are in pain and therefore not healed. Our bodies demand that we confess sickness rather than health. While we are controlled by the flesh, we have great difficulty confessing health in the face of pain. But while controlled by our spirits, sickness cannot stay unless we allow it!

Reference to the spirit here is spelt with a small "s". Isn't it the Spirit of God that should control us and not our own spirits? Can we really trust our spirits to keep us in check? We most certainly can! It was God's idea to make us one with His Spirit. May I remind you that our spirits cannot be corrupted by sin—we were born of incorruptible seed (1 Peter 1:23).

Knowing our authority and godly identity has some wonderful spin-offs:

- Living out kingly character becomes the new norm.
- A godly self-image leads to healthy self-respect.
- Self-value enables us to value others more highly.
- We cease to seek attention—we have our Father's approval.
- A closer relationship makes for intimacy in worship.

- The closer, the more awesome His glory.
- His glory leads to humility.
- We shine—the glory of sonship is upon us.
- The miraculous becomes the new norm.
- We see the enemy as a defeated foe.

Our Deepest Fear

Marianne Williamson © A Return to Love

Our deepest fear is not that we are inadequate.
Our deepest fear is that we are powerful beyond measure.
It is our light, not our darkness that most frightens us.
We ask ourselves, who am I to be brilliant?
Actually, who are you not to be?
You are a child of God.
Your playing small does not serve the world.
There's nothing enlightened about shrinking so that other people
won't feel insecure around you.
We are all meant to shine, as children do.
We were born to make manifest the glory of God that is within us.
It's not just in some of us; it's in every believer.
And as we let our own light shine, we unconsciously give other
people permission to do the same.
As we're liberated from our own fear, our presence automatically
liberates others.

Note: Third last line altered from "everyone" to "every believer".

Repentance

Why is repentance such a scary word? Repentance seems like we have to give up something, lose something. It's the word we would rather not hear. Maybe it frightens us because we have to admit that we are wrong, or perhaps after trying many times we have slipped back as many times. Like new years' resolutions, our best intensions have faded over time. If we haven't managed to keep the promises we have made to ourselves, why would we believe that additional promise making would be any different? There's no joy in it; just disappointment for letting ourselves down, so we stop repenting.

Give it a thought: Would God really expect us to do something that's practically guaranteed to fail? Would He want us to lose our joy, as we beat ourselves half to death with guilt and shame? Can you honestly imagine Him enjoying our despair? If depression and despair is all that repentance can produce, then maybe our concept of repentance isn't what God had in mind.

If repentance is a matter of placing the burden of change upon ourselves, a matter of behavioural modification by sheer grit and determination, then where does God fit into the equation? Surely Christianity offers us more hope than the power of our fickle resolve to change ourselves? Isn't Christianity about operating at a level of power far greater than our own?

If we are failing to resist temptations, then it is obvious that we are using human resolve, while the divine power at our disposal lies dormant. In that case, how should we approach repentance? As always, God has the answer. He doesn't want us to repent FROM sin, He wants us to repent TOWARDS Him. "Testifying both to the Jews, and also to the Greeks, repentance TOWARD God, and faith TOWARD our Lord Jesus Christ" (Act 20:21 KJV).

Why is direction important when repenting? When we repent from sin, we are doing it in our strength, but when we repent towards God, we are doing it in His strength. We don't have to give up anything. He simply changes what our hearts enjoy doing. When the passion for the iniquity ceases, we lose interest in the iniquity. Offensive behaviour is nothing more than a product of offensive thinking. Once our thinking has been adjusted, our actions need no further attention. Let's face it, we have tried it all before—striving just doesn't work! But then again, when we follow God's instructions, striving is entirely unnecessary.

Repentance is a matter of allowing God to reverse our thinking. A good starting point would be to examine our concept of God. If we perceive Him to be an austere judge, ready to convict and chide us for infringing religious rules, then rather than progress, we will regress into guilt, gloom and despair! So, to avoid yet another round of shame, we're likely to avoid facing another ineffective repentance. But there is no need for such destructive emotions. If we can grasp just how understanding and loving our Papa really is, we will welcome every opportunity to repent—knowing that His care and concern comes without judgement. Thankfully, He doesn't use condemnation; He uses guidance, coaxing us upward and onward to better things! *It's His goodness and kindness that lead to repentance!*" (Rom 2:4)

"Well," you may be saying, "Doesn't the Holy Spirit convict us of sin?" You are not the only one to believe this. In all my years of church going, this was drummed into my head. I was taught that if I was feeling condemned over an issue, it was the work of Satan. However, if I was feeling convicted, it was the work of the Holy Spirit. Trouble was, I had no way of distinguishing the difference between the two feelings—was this Satan or the Holy Spirit? Either way, I just fell into the grip of regret and self-condemnation.

Well what does scripture have to say on this point?

"When he comes, he will convict the world of sin, righteousness, and judgment" (John 16:8).

"Well there it is Deon; it definitely says that He will convict us." Read the passage again and this time look out for "who" it is that He will convict. Is it the world (the unbeliever) or is it the believer? It is *"the world"*. He is not saying that He will convict believers. "Now Deon, that's stretching it, we are all of the world." Sure, we are, but the next verse clarifies who in the world He is referring to—it's those who *"do not believe in me"* (John 16:9).

It couldn't be clearer—in this scripture He is very specific about which group the Holy Spirit convicts—it is unbelievers!

"Deon, you are really splitting hairs here. Even if He doesn't specifically mention it, we have all felt conviction from time to time."

Unquestionably, yes! But who is accusing us? There is one who has earned the reputation of *"accuser of the brethren"*, better known as Satan. He has assigned his messengers to keep us feeling bad about ourselves to the point of shame. When we buy into His accusations, guilt comes with a sense of unworthiness. In this condition it is difficult to believe that God would want to favour us.

The Question still begs an answer. If the Holy Spirit does not convict us, then what part does the Spirit play in keeping us on the straight and narrow? Verse 13 of the same chapter has the answer. *"Yet when the Spirit of Truth comes, he will GUIDE you into all truth. For he will not speak on his own accord, but will speak whatever he hears and will declare to you the things that are to come"* (John 16:13).

Wow! How wonderful is that! The Holy Spirit doesn't convict us; He *"guides"* us. Although not convicting us "from" sin; He is guiding us *"into"* all truth. There is no need to be led from sin when we are being guided towards truth. If He were to lead us "from" sin, we would be preoccupied with the wrong thing (sin). His way is far better! In steering our meditation towards our Christlikeness, rather than towards our weaknesses, we magnify the solution rather than the problem. He is out to adjust our focus!

The truth about ourselves, is that we are *"the righteousness of God in Christ"*. The truth about sin is that it has been dealt with in full—God has no record of it. The truth about Old Covenant law, is that it does not apply to New Covenant believers (Eph 2:15).

The truth about God is that His love for us is never contingent upon personal performance. Another truth about our sins, whether past, present or future, is that God does not impute them to us, He has already imputed them to Jesus (Rom 4:8). The Father has already found Jesus guilty and executed Him for all our past, present and future sins. The Holy Spirit couldn't possibly find anything else for which to convict us. Rather than convict us, He has chosen to guide us, leading us towards godliness. How liberating—what a relief!

The Holy Spirit is our compass, always pointing northwards as He leads us into all truth. Condemnation is the work of our enemy, always pointing southwards, reminding us of our inadequacies and failures. When we turn east or west, the Holy Spirit doesn't convict us, because that would turn us southwards and get us obsessed with sin. No, He beckons us northwards; guiding us towards truth and godliness.

Conviction works with negatives, leading to self-recrimination—a sure way to fall into even more sin. Conversely, guidance works with positives, leading to godly living.

I can only imagine how hurtful it must be for a Father to hear His very own children blaming Him for something He didn't do, while the real culprit, the accuser of the brethren, gets off scot free—how shameful of us? We have given The Holy Spirit a bad rap for far too long—in the process we have damaged our self-esteem and cancelled our faith—prayer disabling actions!

The truth is that God is too holy to convict two people of the same crime. If He has already convicted Jesus for all our crimes, whether past, present or future, how could He possibly convict us as well?

The Holy Spirit is our inner GPS. Rather than telling us where we have gone wrong, He tells us the right way to go. With GPS, when we miss the turn-off, it immediately replots a new route, always showing us the way forward, never chiding us for making wrong turns. GPS is patient with the very worst of navigators—never getting angry when we fail to follow its instructions. Similarly, the Holy Spirit always leads from the front with guidance, while Satan continues to lead from behind with accusations.

My son-in-law's GPS has a lady's voice calling out street directions—he calls her Emily. He talks back to Emily as though she is a real person. At times, when he thinks he knows a better route, he argues with her and can sometimes get pretty mean with her. Despite this, she never retaliates. If he chooses a wrong route, she simply calls out another route that will get him out of his self-inflicted pickle. Never does she tell him that he is a bad navigator. Even when his obstinate resistance to her patient instructions lands him down cal-de-sacs with no way out, she doesn't say, "I could have told you so?" No, she calmly plots yet another route.

The Holy Spirit is our guiding light, our GPS—infinitely more gracious than any manmade Satellite Guidance Systems. He guides us forwards to godliness rather than chiding us with conviction—reminding us of who we are in Christ, rather than of who we are in our sin. Every time we blame the Holy Spirit for Satan's accusations, we are maligning His fine character. When our right standing with God is brought into question, our prayers are brought into question. Unworthiness is a sure way to undermine our confidence in prayer.

So, how do we explain the twinges of conscience that everyone experiences from time to time? *"(..It might not be a matter of conscience for you, but it is for the other person.) For why should my freedom be limited by what someone else thinks?"* (1 Cor 10:29).

Have you noticed that each believer's conscience has unique and different values? One believer may be comfortable with something that would deeply trouble another. Paul's conscience allowed Him to eat food offered to idols, but less mature believers were offended by this. If the Holy Spirit only has one level of holiness, then the different levels of conscience experienced by Paul and other believers was certainly not the Holy Spirit's conviction; it can only be put down to each person's unique conscience. The Holy Spirit doesn't have varying standards, whereas each person's conscience has its own sense of right and wrong.

We had consciences long before we got the Holy Spirit. In fact, all unbelievers have consciences, even if they choose to ignore them. Consciences are moulded out of life's experiences—each person developing different values, unique to themselves.

An American ministry team of ladies went on an outreach to Germany. A welcoming church function was arranged by the German ladies. The American ladies were extremely well dressed and well groomed. The German ladies were so shocked to see makeup on their faces that they wept, and their tears ran down their faces and dripped into their beer.

Here are two cultures, neither one understanding the other. The Germans were offended by the make-up on the Americans' faces, while the

Americans were offended by the beer the Germans were so brazenly drinking at a church function. Both groups had the same Holy Spirit, but each group had different values of conscience. Obviously, neither of their values were Holy Spirit values.

A stab of conscience is not necessarily a stab of Holy Spirit conviction. Other than the non-negotiable absolutes in the word of God, we are instructed to allow our consciences to guide us regarding unspecified matters. In these cases, we are to submit to these inner twinges—taking care not to sear our consciences. One believer may regard another believer's liberty as sin, but the other believer may conclude that the one judging him needs to discover the liberty of Jesus. We are not to confuse our consciences with the work of the Holy Spirit.

Yes, but what about conviction of judgement? *"...and (convict) of judgment, because the ruler of this world has been judged"* (John 16:11). Continuing with the subject of conviction, Jesus goes on to say that when the Holy Spirit convicts unbelievers of judgement, He is not even talking about judgement upon them. He is referring to the judgement of the ruler of this world, namely Satan. God never intended for us to be judgement conscious. God does not judge us—He has reserved that for the end of days. We are not meant to be conviction and condemnation conscious; we are meant to be conscious of our in Christlikeness, liberty, righteousness and freedom.

"(convict) of righteousness, because I am going to the Father and you will no longer see me" (John 16:10). God is not trying to get us to fixate upon our sins, He wants us to fixate upon our righteousness. We are not the same sinful people that we once were; we are new creatures, a brand-new species of being. If we are under the impression that the Holy Spirit would stoop to Satan's level of accusing the brethren, then we will become preoccupied with our sin, rather than with our righteousness. Sadly, this is what much of the Church is preoccupied with. We still hear questions

such as: "Will God punish me for arguing with my wife?" People still think this way despite the good news (gospel), being regularly taught.

Jessie du Plantis was either taken up into heaven or he saw a vision, he cannot tell the difference. He saw little spirits coming out of God the Father, pleading to be sent into the bodies of newly born-again people. If God gives birth to our new spirits, then we are a lot more like Him than we may have been led to believe. Our spirits are truly brand new at rebirth. Nothing from our old self was carried forward into our new self— everything is entirely new. But it is obvious that our bodies and minds remained unchanged, carrying the same scars as before. The new person we have become is a spirit that only existed in God before He gave birth to us. How lovely to know that we start our rebirth entirely sinless and remain entirely sinless for all time and eternity.

Sin

Law keepers are easy targets for Satan. He knows that no amount of striving can make a person right with God. All he has to do is to convince us to keep striving. Then when we fail to meet the law's exemplary standard, as we inevitably do, it's a simple matter for him to knock us off at will. Guilt and condemnation will take us out at the knees. Beware! Law keeping opens the door to Satan's mischief!

Have you ever watched National Geographic's TV footage of bears standing on rocks in rivers above rapids? The trout innocently leap out of the water to scale the rocks, not realising that they are leaping directly into the mouths of bears. Fresh trout are delicacies to bears. In the same way, innocent law keepers leap straight into Satan's clutches every time they try to keep the law. Law keeping doesn't scare Satan; it gives him all the more grounds upon which to lay accusations. Then he watches with glee as we blame the Holy Spirit for his dirty work, as we say, "the Holy Spirit convicted me". He is a past master at getting Christians to defame the Holy Spirit.

It is a popular teaching that our sins can stand in the way of answered prayer. When those who hold to this belief are challenged by the fact that no person on the face of the planet, whether Christian or not, are without sin, they assert that there is sin and there is SIN. Habitual sin is said to be more prayer blocking than other sins. Others make a distinction between wilful sin and other sins. But all sin is done wilfully. Despite not being able to substantiate their view from the scriptures, they doggedly insist that it is so.

How else can they explain away unanswered prayer? They are unlikely to admit that they have failed to pray with the kind of emphatic faith that always gets results. James is clear on this, "wait and see" prayers are too wishy-washy to get results! People who are not convinced of their authority as sons, are unlikely to stand in unwavering faith when prayers seem to go unanswered. Let's face it, it takes faith of the unshakable kind to move mountains!

Another reason for unanswered prayer could be that we are calling on God to take care of something that He has clearly authorised us to take care of. Or it could be that we are praying against a person, when we ought to be blessing the person and binding the spirit responsible for that person's repulsive actions. Satan and his cohorts, are seldom recognized as the real perpetrators!

Unforgiveness is a killer. Dennis Collins, a friend of mine in the Jewellery business, sold an exceptionally large diamond to a visiting American purely on the basis of trust. He promised Dennis that he would arrange payment immediately upon his return to the USA. Weeks turned into months and months into years without any sign of a payment. The amount involved was large enough to cause Dennis considerable concern. He did his best to trace the individual, but without success. The man was a Mormon, so Dennis tried to obtain his contact details through Mormon HQ in Salt Lake City, but their policy of confidentiality did not allow for such disclosures.

One cannot blame Dennis for bearing unforgiveness—his trust had been seriously abused. He had prayed and taken all the normal faith steps without success. What was he to do?

Eighteen years later, at the point of sheer exasperation, the Lord showed him that he needed to forgive the man, count the debt as a seed sown to God and move on with his life. Though Dennis was tempted to make one final last-ditch attempt before throwing in the towel, he obediently decided to write-off the debt, forgive the man and get on with his life.

That is not where the story ends. Shortly thereafter, entirely out of the blue, Dennis got news from the man. He was transferring double the outstanding amount to Dennis in US dollars. Over a period of eighteen years, the exchange rate between the South African currency and the US dollar had changed in Dennis' favour—he received double payment multiplied by five times as much in South African Rands—a total of ten times more than was owed. What brought about the release? Nothing but forgiveness! It turned a debt into a seed, and the seed turned into an enormous harvest.

People often say that God sometimes says no to our prayers. Sure, God will choose whether to say "yes or no" when praying for direction on a matter. This is not the kind of prayer that we are dealing with here. If you pray for something specific and you are of the opinion that God may say no to your request, then you will not be able to say with emphatic certainty that you received your answer at the precise moment that you prayed for it. If we feel that we can't know with any degree of certainty, then our faith is wavering between certainty and uncertainty. James says that such prayers will not be answered (Jas 1:6,7). If we can't believe that we have received the desired outcome while in the very process of uttering our prayers, then we are not practising faith; we are practising wishful thinking. We must admit that we do not believe Jesus' words in Mark 11:24. *"Therefore I say unto you, what things soever ye desire, when ye pray, believe that ye receive them, and ye shall have them"* (KJV).

We can't have it both ways. We have to make up our minds on this issue. If the answer to our prayer can be "no", then Jesus lied in Mark 11:24. In this key scripture, did Jesus say that we could only expect certain things that He would allow or not allow? Read it again. Did He say we can have anything "God desires" or did He say that we can have anything "we desire"? According to this verse, we are specifically asked to pray for "our" desires; not "His". Sometimes we pray, "I will have whatever you desire, Lord." Sounds very pious and humble, but God replies, "I desire whatever you desire for yourself."

"No, Deon, that would lead to praying for all kinds of sinful desires, like wanting to have somebody else's wife." Really! That's a crazy notion. We know that God cannot be an accessory to anything sinful. If we are spirit-led, we are not going to ask God to aid and abet us in sinful pursuits. God doesn't choose not to sin; He is quite simply incapable of sinning. Are we really going to expect Him to come and sin with us? Let's not kid ourselves!

If we are making a sinful request of a God who is holy, how would we have the courage to say with emphatic certainty that our prayers will be answered? David put it this way, *"If I regard iniquity in my heart, the Lord will not hear me"* (Psalm 66:18). From this verse you may conclude that if there is sin in your life, you cannot have your prayers answered. Well, that can't be true. All people have sin in their lives. The Bible says that all have sinned and fallen short of the glory of God (Rom 3:23). There is not one righteous, no, not one! (Rom 3:10). Surely David wasn't saying that God won't answer his prayers unless he is perfect. I believe he was saying that God will not be a party to answering a prayer that would require God to compromise His holiness.

At a home church meeting, one of the ladies expressed her impatience with taxi drivers. In our city, they are a law unto themselves, taking liberties, breaking traffic laws without giving the slightest thought to the safety of other commuters. Every morning on her way to work, she would stew in her frustration, blood boiling with extreme irritation, never giving them an inch on the road.

This was a respected godly woman, full of love for others and highly regarded for her understanding of God's word. Would you say that this sin would cancel her prayers? "No", you may say, "These are simply harmless frustrations that we all experience from time to time." Perhaps you feel that only habitual or wilful sins get in the way of prayer. Really? Well then, aren't her sins habitual and wilful? Of course they are, and we have all been there and done that. The truth is that all of us habitually and wilfully sin. The Bible makes no distinction between non-habitual sin and habitual sin, or between wilful and non-wilful sin. It doesn't even distinguish between small sins and big sins. Jesus said that even an impure thought makes us guilty, regardless of whether we act on it or not. Paul said that if we are guilty of breaking one law, we are guilty of all the law. We are either 100% pure or 100% impure—there are no degrees to it.

Fortunately, it wasn't our behaviour that made us 100% pure, it was our rebirth. Our positional righteousness in Christ is never in question. But where the rubber hits the road, it is not the same. How do we cope in an imperfect world? In our daily encounters, decisions are made on the hop, and nobody is immune from faux pas.

Why is the process of behavioural sanctification ongoing and continuous? Why is there no end to it? The answer is plain—nobody actually reaches the point of practical perfection this side of eternity. In that case, those who teach that God does not answer prayer when there is sin in a person's life, have not only robbed others of God's favour; they have also consigned their own prayers to naught. If per chance they were right, then nobody's prayers could ever be answered!

Well, that is just not so! The truth is that Jesus never taught that sin had anything whatsoever to do with unanswered prayer. When Jesus walked this planet, He never once told a single person to forsake sin before he or she could be healed. If sin could cancel prayer, then Jesus was way out of line—He gave healing to everyone who asked for it. It wasn't the sin of the people of Nazareth that prevented them from receiving miracles from Jesus, it was their unbelief—but then again, unbelief is what sin is.

"When Jesus returned to Capernaum, a Roman officer came and pleaded with Him, "Lord, my young servant lies in bed, paralyzed and in terrible pain." Jesus said, "I will come and heal him." But the officer said, "Lord, I am not worthy to have You come into my home. Just say the word from where You are, and my servant will be healed. I know this because I am under the authority of my superior officers, and I have authority over my soldiers. I only need to say, 'Go,' and they go, or 'Come,' and they come. And if I say to my slaves, 'Do this,' they do it." When Jesus heard this, He was amazed. Turning to those who were following Him, He said, "I tell you the truth, I haven't seen faith like this in all Israel!"" (Mat 8:5-10).

Jesus spoke of great faith and little faith. Ever tried walking on water? Anybody with a basic knowledge of physics will tell you that it is not even vaguely in the realm of possibility! But that didn't stop Peter. But even after such a remarkable feat, Jesus did not hand him the trophy for the greatest faith—no, He chided him for his little faith! Seriously? I mean seriously? The man walked on water, for goodness sake! Jesus, are You saying that Peter's amazing gravity defeating achievement takes little faith?

The prize for the greatest faith didn't even go to one of Jesus' disciples, nor did it go to a fastidious law keeping Pharisee; it went to a non-law keeping despised Roman! Romans were pagans, outside of the family of God. When he asked Jesus to heal his servant, Jesus didn't first lead him in a prayer of repentance, nor did He look down his nose upon him with religious contempt. To the contrary, the centurion's faith got the highest compliment recorded in scripture. Jesus was amazed at his faith! He called it the greatest faith he had ever encountered! If, as some would have it, we must be current with repentance to have our prayers answered, then Jesus should have turned this pagan away with contempt. After all, he even admitted to being unworthy. He said it in so many words, *"Lord, I am not worthy to have You come into my home"*. This being the case, should we really be allowing feelings of unworthiness to stand in the way of our prayers? Besides his sin, not even the centurion's offbeat religion could block his prayer. Imagine that! If a pagan could have his prayer answered without repentance, then anybody, from the vilest offender to the sweetest Christian offender can take heart—their prayers can be answered without repentance. Are you finding this difficult accept? The thought of such grace doesn't usually go down too well with religious people! But thankfully it doesn't end there. The goodness of God has a wonderful way of leading us into repentance (Rom 2:4).

It's not our sins; it's our unbelief that blocks our prayers. But of course, that is not a good reason to carry on sinning. When we become aware of our sin, it behoves us to repent before suffering sin's ghastly consequences. Let's not kid ourselves! If we dabble with sin, we'll be required to pay its wages, and it's always going to be more than we would want to pay. Although God does not punish us for sinning, sin comes with its own consequences. And none of them are pretty.

If you are basing your faith upon your practical righteousness, you'll always be hesitant in believing. Uncertainty robs faith of its power.

Uncertainty exists in the realm of doubt and unbelief, and nothing is more faith debilitating than doubt. James said that the person whose faith wavers must not think that he will receive anything (James 1:6,7). If our prayers are of the wavering type, why even bother to pray? Scripture is clear on this—failure is guaranteed! We simply cannot afford to waver an inch in believing for the desired outcome of our prayers. If we are serious about getting our prayers answered, we had better believe with emphatic certainty that they have been answered, not at some undefined date in the future, but at the precise moment of uttering them! Any other concept that goes by the name of faith is not faith at all! Faith declares miracles into existence without a single thread of evidence to support such confidence!

You may say that you have had prayers answered without the slightest hint of faith on your part. You may say that that proves God is sovereign and can do whatever He wants, whenever He wants. No, that is not what it proves. God must have somebody's faith to work with. If not yours, someday else's

If that is the case, is it okay to throw righteousness out of the window and live like the world? That's not what Jesus taught. He said that we are to *"seek his righteousness"* (Mat 6:33). While earnestly seeking His righteousness, we remain patently aware that we are not going to achieve perfection this side of eternity. But take heart, our lack of perfection is not a prayer-blocker—it's not our perfection that gets God's attention, it's our faith!

Keeping God Happy

Have you seen the T-shirt that reads: "Jesus is coming—Look busy?" It is meant to be a joke, but judging by all the religious buzzing about, it is clear that believers often get caught up in the hubbub of church activities! But trying to look busy does not impress God. We forget that our good works are as filthy rags to Him. Actually, a more accurate translation is "soiled menstruation rags". In the culture of the day, menstruation made women unclean—their rags were treated with disgust. In using such derogatory language, Isaiah came close to swearing. That's how serious he was about God's revulsion for our piffling efforts to be holy. Let's face it, we cannot impress God. I am sure that religious pretending and pious preening is just as nauseating Him as it is to us!

So many saintly believers sincerely go out of their way, striving to keep God happy with good works and law keeping. Unfortunately, our very best works, though commendable, don't win brownie points with God. Looking busy for Jesus might impress church oversight, but that's as far as it goes.

Now faith that rests on the finished work of the cross is different— not sometimes up and sometimes down—it stands on something that is forever established in unquestionable certainty. Of course, good works are good, but if they are done to make ourselves right with God, they cut us off from Christ and cancel God's grace in our lives. *"For if you are trying to make yourselves right with God by keeping the law, you have been cut off from Christ! You have fallen away from God's grace"* (Gal 5:4).

Must we stop doing good works then? Well of course not! If they are not done to attain divine acceptance, they have value. Truth is, we already have divine acceptance and therefore are empowered to do the works of Jesus. Religious flitting about may make us look good, but that's all it can do!

"The Spirit gives life, the flesh profits nothing" (John 6:63). There is no point in striving to produce good works in an effort to get into God's good books. They are works of the flesh! James 2:10 warns *"For whosoever shall keep the whole law, and yet offend in one point, he is guilty of all"* (KJV). Seeing that no man in the history of mankind has ever managed to keep all the law, even the best law keeper is no less guilty than the worst law keeper. Or, to put it another way, in God's sight the best law keeper is as guilty as the terrorists responsible for the deaths of thousands of innocent moms and dads on 9/11. Even if we have successfully kept "most" of the law, we remain as guilty as a paedophile or a murderer in God's estimation. Law keeping does not possess the power to keep us saved, or for that matter, to earn God's favour.

The law was not given to facilitate reconciliation with God. To the contrary, it was given to show us how far we are from being reconciled with Him. It demonstrates the impossibility of attaining God's impeccable standard. We must seek another solution—a solution that excludes flawed strivings—a solution that only a saviour can bring!

We are called to view ourselves in God's mirror. But those who mistakenly believe the mirror to be the law, discover their sinfulness, when they ought to be discovering their unblemishable state of righteousness! Although the law reveals their problems, it offers no solution to their problem. Not to despair, God has provided the perfect solution—it's called grace!

So, you may have messed up big time and be living in the chaos of your own making. Well, the good news is that you don't have to have it all together in order to gain God's favour. It is because you are incapable of making yourself right that He extends grace to you! If your life is one long battle of unfixable regrets, turn them over to God. Nobody can push toothpaste back into the tube! God says, "Stop striving—toss the old tube—here's a brand new one—it's free of charge—Jesus paid for it in full".

In Islam you are okay as long as the good you do outweighs the bad. They are under the illusion that heaven can be earned. If we as Christians, have any aspirations of getting to heaven by good works and holiness, we might as well convert to Islam. At least good works count for something with their god. Unfortunately, in Islam there is no grace for the sin problem. In the same way that Islam's good works cannot save them, neither can Christian good works save us. And keeping Old Covenant law won't get us there either. It's either grace alone, with absolutely no credits added for keeping the law, or we are not saved at all! *"If God's promise is only for those who obey the law, then faith is not necessary and the promise is pointless. For the law always brings punishment on those who try to obey it. (The only way to avoid breaking the law is to have no law to break!)"* (Rom 4:14-15).

God has told us how to live by His favour. Despite this, good works and holiness are still being taught by well-meaning Bible teachers as a means of gaining more of God's favour. How sad to spend a lifetime climbing a ladder, only to discover that our ladder had been leaning against the wrong wall. Trying to obtain God's favour through good works will get us nowhere!

Heavenly maths:

- Faith in Jesus + grace = salvation + favour + relationship.
- Faith in Jesus + anything else = nothing at all.
- Faith in Jesus + OT law keeping = cancelled faith + cancelled grace.

Any kind of good works that we deem necessary to add to the blood of Jesus, negates, no, completely cancels grace! We must decide what our salvation stands on. Is it grace or is it works? If we were to believe that it should be a little of each, then we would only be as secure as the weaker of the two, and there are no prizes for guessing which that would be. Let's face it, if works were required to keep us saved, how awfully flimsy our salvation would be!

The problem with keeping the law is that it is not like taking a high school exam where a 40% score would be enough to get us through. With the law, even a 99% score is not enough. It has to be 100% all the time. No-one in the history of mankind has ever achieved a perfect score, and you and I are not going to be the first to achieve it. That being the case, why bother striving for something that is guaranteed to cancel our grace?

Why was grace given in the first place? If it were possible to successfully keep all the commandments, there would have been no need for it. Grace was specifically established because, no matter how hard we may try, successful law keeping is simply not in the realm of human possibility. Grace was designed specifically to take our fallibility into account. We cannot make ourselves right through law keeping. But no need to despair, grace is enough!

Conclusion

Frankie found life at the swamp very trying. Leo the Lion was in charge of the jungle, so why didn't he just step in and help the hapless little frog out? Leo couldn't be blamed for the dangers there. If it wasn't the weather, it was the foxes, hawks, and snakes. Worse still, that sneaky Stevie was up to his tricks as usual. More than that, Leo could not be blamed for Frankie's silly mistakes.

Frankie Frog wanted his puddle paradise back, but Stevie the snake wasn't going to give it back without a fight, and he didn't fight fair. Frankie wasn't prepared to take Stevie on—snakes eat frogs. Frankie would have to be as strong as a lion—how he wished he could be a lion!

Leo, king of the jungle, really wanted to help Frankie out, but it wasn't His territory. Then Leo came up with a solution. He would send his cub to enter Stevie's territory, take Stevie on and die in the process from a venomous bite from Stevie. He would do it all for Frankie's sake. But his cub would recover and defeat Stevie, thus restoring Frankie to his rightful place. He would allow Frankie to share his kingly identity. With a spirit and mind-set of a king, Frankie would rule the puddle with overwhelming authority—Stevie would be no match for him.

With the heart of a lion, Frankie was more than equal to the task of regaining his kingdom and ruling his puddle with decisive authority! Stevie continued with his old tricks of fear and intimidation. Sometimes Frankie would forget his new lion identity. Stevie was quick to seize upon any opportunity to frighten Frankie—at times scaring him witless and then feeding off his fear. Frankie's words of doubt and unbelief were enough to give Stevie the right to wreak havoc in his little world.

Then Frankie would remind himself of his lion heartedness. With his princely identity, Frankie had the courage to take Stevie on and put him in his place as only a lion can.

Frankie also discovered that, as a lion, he could relate one on one with Leo—something he could not do as a frog. They became very close, able to share their most intimate thoughts.

Even though we may not be prepared to admit it, we cannot deny that it is nice to have others think well of us. When we look the part and all they see of us are our successes, who can blame them for admiring us— the illusion suits us. But such social posturing doesn't cut it with God.

As sons and daughters, we take after Dad; He is always in control of His domain. As much as we would like to be in control of ours, in truth, if we have left spiritual matters in the hands of professional father figures, we have forfeited our personal authority. When they get it wrong; we get it wrong. Their misunderstandings become our misunderstandings.

There are many challenges to our domain—they come at us from every which way—at times we don't even see them coming. Sadly, ignorance of our true identity and the authority that comes with it, becomes Satan's opportunity.

Some challenges are in direct response to our bad decisions, but most of them are just plain curve balls that life throws our way. We're often caught off guard. Who is responsible for the chaos? We can't blame Satan for all of them, but his hands are certainly not clean.

Who done it? Agatha Christie had us guessing. Was it the butler or the chambermaid? Is God responsible for the chaos that we often find ourselves in? Let's put this quandary to the test: Does it fit in with His integrity and holy character? Not likely! The more we understand about the character of Jesus, the more we understand about the character of our Father—He is not one iota less gracious than His Son.

Who done it? Was it Satan, ourselves, nature or maybe God? It could be any of the above except God. Of this one thing we can be certain, God is innocent, He is definitely not to blame! If ever there was a dead cert, it is this!

We often hear Christians explaining why bad things happen to good people. They say, *"My thoughts,"* says the LORD, *"are not like yours, and my ways are different from yours"* (Isa 55: 8). In this way they are saying that we shouldn't question God's big plan, because His thoughts are too high for mortals to understand. But in saying this, was God really telling us that He has some kind of superior motive for hurting us? As always, we only get half the truth when we quote half the scripture. When read in context with the preceding verse it becomes clear that this is not what Isaiah is saying. It starts this way *"Let the wicked leave their way of life and change their way of thinking. Let them turn to the LORD, our God; he is merciful and quick to forgive"* (Isa 55:7). That throws a very different light on what He is telling us. It is to forsake our thinking, because it is wicked thinking, and adopt His thinking, because it is higher thinking. He is not saying that we will never be able to understand His thoughts. To the contrary, He is calling on us to think His higher thoughts because we will benefit from them!

This scripture should not be used to explain that God puts stuff on us that should not be questioned because His ways are too advanced for us to understand. Again, by blaming God, we are letting Satan off the hook. It is his evil agenda—he'll do anything to induce an element of doubt to our confidence—he can't afford to have us participating in God's generosity.

Surely God could not possibly be pleased with being falsely accused by His beloved children. In misquoting this verse, we infer that God is guilty of carrying out Satan's agenda—making Him out to be unholy!

I am sure that we all know that our thinking is not always what it should be. When we take offence, we are plain and simply judging, and when we are judgemental, we are definitely not thinking His higher thoughts. And when we feel defeated, it should be obvious that we are not thinking His higher thoughts. To think His thoughts, is to ooze with confidence—resolute in convictions and unshakable in faith! Stress and despair are no match for His thoughts—a mindset that lifts spirits, engenders joy and calms cares! No matter how terrible the storm; no matter how turbulent the waves, life-buoys stay afloat!

Who do you think you are? We have all been asked this question, usually in admonishment for overstepping other people's boundaries. But this is a pertinent question. WHO DO YOU THINK YOU ARE? Your answer will determine how you fare over life's hurdles. The hurdles are not optional, you will definitely encounter them on life's athletic track, but whether you leap over them or trip over them, will for the most part depend on who you think you are. For as a man thinks in his heart, so is he. If you think you are in the god-class as a son of the living God, the hurdles and curve balls will not intimidate you. Knowing who you are gives you an attitude, a cockiness to take on Satan and any curve balls he may chuck your way. However terrible the circumstances, they will be no match for your incontestable in Christ-ness!

James Bond ordered his Martini "shaken, not stirred". That's what God wants for His children: "Shaken, yes, but not stirred". Life's misfortunes may shake us, but our faith remains unstirred and unmoved.

We know our identity, and that's enough to put us way over and above any adversity!

Deon and Susan Stevens

Meet Me in the Stairwell

Author unknown

You say you will never forget where you were when
you heard the news On September 11, 2001.
Neither will I.

I was on the 110th floor in a smoke filled room
with a man who called his wife to say, "Good-Bye". I
held his fingers steady as he dialled. I gave him the
peace to say, "Honey, I am not going to make it, but it
is OK. I am ready to go".

I was with his wife when he called as she fed
breakfast to their children. I held her up as she
tried to understand his words and as she realized
he wasn't coming home that night.

I was in the stairwell of the 23rd floor when a
woman cried out to Me for help. "I have been
knocking on the door of your heart for 50 years!" I said.
"Of course I will show you the way home—only
believe in Me now".

I was at the base of the building with the Priest
ministering to the injured and devastated souls.
I took him home to tend to his Flock in Heaven. He
heard my voice and answered.

I was on all four of those planes, in every seat,
with every prayer. I was with the crew as they
were overtaken. I was in the very hearts of the
believers there, comforting and assuring them that their
faith has saved them.

I was in Texas, Virginia, California, Michigan, Afghanistan.
I was standing next to you when you heard the terrible news.
Did you sense Me?

I want you to know that I saw every face. I knew
every name—though not all know Me. Some met Me
for the first time on the 86th floor.

Some sought Me with their last breath.
Some couldn't hear Me calling to them through the
smoke and flames; "Come to Me... this way... take
My hand". Some chose, for the final time, to ignore Me.
But, I was there.

I did not place you in the Tower that day. You
may not know why, but I do. However, if you were
there in that explosive moment in time, would you have
reached for Me?

Sept. 11, 2001, was not the end of the journey
for you. But someday your journey will end. And I
will be there for you as well. Seek Me now while I may
be found. Then, at any moment, you know you are
"ready to go".
I will be in the stairwell of your final moments.

Also by this Author:

Grace, the most treasured gift of all is under fire from a most unlikely foe—Christendom itself! Grace is often perceived to be at odds with holiness. But it takes more than good intentions to achieve holiness—it takes love! Holiness is love in action, and we have no better example of it than in God's grace. Sadly, when Christendom reduces grace, it reduces our redemption.

"In Christ", we are so much more than mere mortals. In reality, we have what Christ has! This knowledge opens the door to enormous possibilities. Although the price for it has been paid in full, we may have to make some mind adjustments to benefit from it. If we were to discover that religion is holding us back from God's best, would we be prepared to walk away from it?

Also by this Author:

Fulfilment in life—the ultimate prize! It is something that one would expect to find in religion. After all, religion makes many promises. But sadly, these claims are often beyond our reach. They are only obtainable through the often maligned, gift of grace.

Jesus is not the founder of a religion; He opposes religion. He made His feelings patently clear—He did not appreciate religiosity—never uttering a single word of accusation to sinful humanity, but never having a single kind word for religious people.

Oodles of fulfilment can be found in grace! Feelings of inferiority and self-doubt simply cannot survive its edification. It inspires faith and godliness, and makes life enormously fulfilling!

Also by this Author:

If you have inherited so much in Christ, why would you continue striving so hard to get it?

He left you wealth, health, peace, joy and so much more—yet you may not have experienced this. Your inheritance did not come to you because of your good works or holiness and therefore cannot be taken away because of your lack thereof. If you insist on working for it, there aren't enough hours in the day for you to do enough to deserve it. You are already in receipt of an immense fortune. Your bountiful inheritance was placed into your personal trust account, available to be withdrawn at your pleasure. Seeing it is already yours—why in the world would you still be striving to get it?

When you discover how highly God esteems you, exactly as you are right now, your self-esteem will get a shot in the arm, boosting your sense of worthiness to appropriate His favour. You are not highly favoured because you are holy but simply because you are His dearly loved child.

Also by this Author:

How is it that eager new believers turn into dreary religious zombies? What is the process that destroys a new believer's free spirit?

Babes in Christ lose their individuality as they are pressed into moulds of religious conformity. Religion is a killer! If religion was a man, he ought to be strung up from the nearest tree.

What is the solution? Realising that we are loved in our present condition without having to make any promises to change is the greatest discovery that a believer can make. God would rather relate to weird and wonderful misfits, oddballs and "characters", than to a whole army of Terracotta Soldiers. Discover the childish wonderment of living loved— not something offered by religion.

Daily Reading:

Believing in God's grace is one thing—a wonderful idea in theory but how do we apply it to our day to day living? Where did we get the idea that God is a small-minded bookkeeper, tallying up our failures and successes on a score sheet?

How you score in life has no bearing on the degree of grace you receive. We are the objects of God's furious love pursuit and we can luxuriate in this liberating knowledge.

If Christians are guilty of anything, it would be navel gazing. So much time is spent with self-introspection, self-recrimination and self-condemnation. Somehow, we have lost sight of the fact that we are made right because of what Jesus did and not because of what we did.

Love Empowering Capsules brings our perspective back to our privileged position of dearly loved children who are fully empowered to lead overcoming and abundant lives brimming with peace and joy.